The Prayers of a

Powerful Praying Princess

My life, triumph & prayers

By Princess Tynika Baker-Isaac

D1570558

Dedication

To my late parents Alicia Faye & Anthony Eugene Sr. for giving me life & loving me the best way you knew how. My late grandmother Leanna Faye who raised me & made me serve at St. James. My husband Alvin for encouraging me to share our story and giving me plenty to pray about, I love you more today than ever you are my best friend. Christian, Davian, Isaiah, & Ezekiel you 4 made me a better person. I love you all more than words. Alexis & Amanda thank you for loving my sons I love you both. My 1st grandchild Isaiah Jr, Nana loves you. My sister-cousins Linda, Marquita, & Angel the picture on the cover represents what we have always been to each other & that's support! I have always been able to be real with you & know that no matter what I say & do you will love me! We are more like sisters than cousins. The picture shows you helping me get my crown straight & I want you to know that if I see your crown slipping I will help straighten it. My Hutcherson, Baker, & Evans families I love each of you! Princess Sheila, you are my sister & I thank God for you. All past, present & future Powerful Praying Princesses you ladies are awesome. Thank you, Princesses Tara, Vernell, Sheila, Ruby & Tamekka for sticking with me on the prayer call through good & bad. Pastor Michael Smith, you are my mentor, confidant, & friend; I thank God for our relationship. Pastor Spence, Elder Coylitia & the GICM family thank you for allowing me to serve the Kingdom of God with you. Bertha, Jane & Vanessa thank you for being the first to read my book I love you ladies. Thank you, Dom C. Willis, the author of Today I! Last but definitely not least to the Lord Jesus Christ for loving me even when I am unlovable & teaching me to love myself. I know I can do all things through You because You strengthen me.

Foreword

In today's world, we allow so many different things to mask the pain. We cover it up with social media, money, new things, etc.... In this book, Tynika Baker-Isaac unveils her life in such a short but organically alluring way that it quickly causes you to identify your own pain, and see the cure in almost the same moment.

Her desire to see women healed and know Jesus Christ, allows the shocking reality of the craziness in this world to be washed away by the power of scripture and prayer. In this book, she shows that every Princess goes through pain, but every Princess has a purpose and a promise that can bring her into position. Continuing in prayer with the Lord will heal those broken places and alleviate the things in our lives that were meant to cause us to stumble. Tynika has moved from one needing care to one giving care and her life details that journey and allows every one of us to have hope in our process on the way to our purpose. Allow Tynika's teaching through life's challenges mentor you to embrace your calling in the midst of personal conflict and struggle.

So get excited about walking with her in this journey of life and experiencing the power and grace of Christ and seeing God walking with you in the journey of your life. I am proud to say that Tynika is still bringing inner healing to hearts!!!

~Pastor Michael Smith

Contents

There are several different types of prayer:

Introduction

Years ago the Lord put on my heart to write a book about my life but I kept procrastinating always questioning myself why anyone would want to read about me. I also knew I wanted to put my prayers and teachings I have written through the years together in a book. I thought; why not combine it all? I am learning to embrace my past, look forward to my future and to be present in my present life.

I truly believe that as women we have to start being real with each other. We often go through the same kinds of hurt but we don't have a strong support system to reach out to because we don't trust other women. We need to support and not judge each other for that to happen we have to be able to trust each other. Yes, I know that to trust someone you have to be vulnerable and when you've been hurt being vulnerable is not easy. I want you to know I've been hurt, broken, let down, abused, used and I still struggle from time to time with low self-esteem, thinking I'm not good enough. But that devil is a liar and I am taking a risk by being vulnerable throughout this book so that I can be free. My prayer is that through reading about some of my pains, struggles, and bad decisions from conception until now that something in my life will connect with a part of your own life. I also pray that I continue to receive healing through writing this book and maybe just maybe it helps you in your process of healing too.....

Let's Pray:

Father in the name of Jesus I come to You asking You to forgive me for all of my sins. Lord anything I have said done or thought that wasn't pleasing to You please forgive me. Lord, I lift up the Princess reading this book and I ask You to touch our emotions that we do not wear them on our sleeve. Help us to get a clear understanding of who we are in You and the love You have for us even though life has been tough. Help us to see that no matter what has happened You have always been there with us. Let us see ourselves the way You see us that we are fearfully and wonderfully made and that we are marvelous because You created us. Father, I ask that something in this book resonates with her spirit and helps her to know she is not alone and somebody is praying for her. I ask You, Lord to bring healing to our memories and the emotions that may come up through me writing this book and her reading this book. Help us to allow ourselves to be vulnerable to You and what You want to do in us. Father, also bring a Holy Spirit- filled God-friend into our lives that will stand, cry, and pray with us when we are going through and also celebrate with us when we get through whatever trials and issues that may arise in our lives in Jesus name I pray, Amen.

What has God told you to do that you haven't finished or that you haven't even begun yet?

_____

_____

_____

_____

_____

_____

_____

_____

_____

_____

_____

_____

_____

_____

Who is Princess Tynika & where did she come from?

I was born to a 15-year-old Alicia (Lisa Faye) and a 17-year-old Anthony (Tony) in Emporia, Kansas. My mother being a scared child hid her pregnancy the entire 9 months. I was told that even after I was born and home from the hospital she still denied having me. My mom's mother raised me and I have no memories of ever living with my mother at a young age. My father came around more than my mom in my childhood because he lived for the most part in Emporia. He did leave to go to the U.S. Navy for a few years and whenever he was in town he would come to pick me up for a visit. I am the only child of my mother and the oldest of 5 children of my father all of us by different women. None of us were raised together, we didn't go to school together and there is a big difference in our ages too. Two of my siblings are young enough to be my children.

Let's Pray:

Father I ask You to touch the heart of Your daughter, give her the strength to feel and be healed from the pains of abandonment and rejection. Lord, help her to see she was wanted, loved and purposed by You. Help her to know that Jesus died for her and would have died even if she was the only person alive. Father, heal the relationship between this Princess and her parents and also the memories of her life. Give her a gift of forgiveness to let go of the disappointment she may feel toward them in Jesus' name, Amen.

*Who are you and where did you come
from?*

_____

_____

_____

_____

_____

_____

_____

_____

_____

_____

_____

_____

_____

_____

_____

_____

1972-1990

My mother left me at a very young age with her mother while she moved around to different states and towns living life and growing up. My grandmother was a mean abusive alcoholic who often would tell me "you ain't shit and you're never going to be shit just like your mother." Grandma whooped all of us but after everyone moved out of the house all of the anger and abuse that we all had shared before was mine alone. I could never understand why she kept me if she hated me so much and I often wished my mom would have put me up for adoption. My grandmother was in a dark place in life. I don't know her whole story and have gotten bits and pieces of it since she died when I questioned her sisters. I remember when I was in elementary school my grandmother had our house painted black. I now can look back and understand why she may have had that done. It was probably because that's how she felt inside. Something has to be seriously broken in a person for them to have their house painted black!

I was raised with my grandmother's two youngest children; my Aunt Phyllis who is 6 years older than me, her older brother and also my 1st cousin my Aunt Terri Ann's daughter Marquita who I call my sister-cousin was in the house off and on. I can remember as far back as head start being molested and raped by my uncle in our home. He would touch me and have me touch him and then later it turned into him raping me which lasted until I was in 4th or 5th grade when he got a steady girlfriend. He was arrested for raping a woman in our home town when I was in the 6th grade. In my grandmother's home children were to "stay in their place" and had no opinion or voice about anything. I guess I thought that was normal because that was the life I lived. Anytime he had to "babysit" me he took the opportunity to do with me what he wanted. There were even times other people were in the house and he would sneak me to a broken down car that was in the back yard or to the basement. I remember once several of us were sitting in the front room one night watching "The Exorcist" and my uncle had me sitting next to him under a blanket touching him. Since getting older and looking back at this I can see how bold and sneaky he was or maybe just how plain stupid he was. But now having matured and received a degree in Psychology I know there were a lot of issues, abuse and other things that happened in my grandmother's house that probably contributed to him being this type of person. I didn't tell anyone about this until I was 15 years old. Richard, my high school sweetheart is the first person I trusted enough to open up to and tell him about the sexual abuse. My uncle would tell me that nobody would believe me and at that time I didn't know it was happening to my sister-cousin too and probably others. I didn't tell my grandmother because I didn't think she would believe me plus she didn't ever want to hear what I had to say anyway. I felt that my uncle was her favorite child.   I feel that somewhere in my mind I thought she already knew and didn't care.

Let's Pray:

Lord in the name of Jesus I ask You to heal the pain and memory of sexual abuse. Heal the pains of not being heard, not having a voice and not having someone to protect the innocence of the Princess reading this book. Father, help this Princess to see that through it all she is still standing because there is purpose in her pain. Lord, give her beauty for her ashes and joy, unspeakable joy. Help her to get the counseling she needs to be able to be mended from the abuse. Help her to be able to forgive the abuser because forgiveness is for her more than for the abuser and also help her to know her self-worth in Jesus' name, Amen.

What happened in your childhood that changed you? Who do you need to forgive? Write them a letter and at the end you have to tell them you forgive them.

_____

_____

_____

_____

_____

_____

_____

_____

_____

_____

_____

_____

_____

Grandma had 9 brothers and sisters and she herself had 7 children so I have a lot of cousins I grew up with. Linda, Angel, and Marquita are my sister-cousins. We spent a lot of time together while growing up. Staying the night at their homes was probably the best part of growing up because their homes were safe places for me. We share so many crazy, good, and bad memories together. My family has been plagued with several generational curses like alcohol and drug addiction, having children out of wedlock and having children at a young age, premature death, and several other curses. I grew up around all of this and was allowed to drink at a very young age. My mother would tell a story about when I was very young she asked me what I wanted for my birthday and I told her a bottle of Riunite wine and a dime lid of weed. This is sad but true. I don't remember the birthday but I do remember she had a picture of me in the park holding a bottle of Riunite wine. I looked about 2 or 3 years old. My mother would come visit me once a year usually around Christmas time and her and my Aunt Terri Ann would always fight then make up and go out to a bar and end up in jail from fighting other people. Please don't get me wrong, I absolutely love my family and thank God that my grandmother kept me and raised me. My life could have been worse especially if my mother would have taken me with her, there's no telling what would have happened to me.

Even though grandma wasn't an affectionate person she did make me feel like my birthdays were a national holiday. She would make my favorite dinner and give me whatever I asked for as a gift. I remember when I was in elementary school and on my birthday all of my classmates and several other children walked home with me from school for my birthday party. To this day birthdays are a big deal to me.

Let's Pray:

Father in the name of Jesus I bind up all generational curses in the family of the Princess reading this prayer. I curse every curse at the root in Jesus' name. Through the authority, Jesus Christ has given me I cancel out the assignment of addiction, premature death, children out of wedlock and all kinds of abuse that are operating in her family. It stops now in Jesus' name! Her children and grandchildren will not suffer from any of the generational curses passed through the bloodline in Jesus' mighty precious name, Amen.

What generational curses do you recognize in your family? Do you know where they started? Write a prayer binding them up in Jesus name.

_____

_____

_____

_____

_____

_____

_____

_____

_____

_____

_____

_____

_____

_____

_____

Aunt Sarah and Uncle Bob's was where we had our family's 4th of July celebration every year when growing up and our house was where we had the weekend parties which both parties consisted of alcohol, drugs, card playing and a fight or two breaking out through the night. My cousins and I had fun playing hide and go seek or catching fire flies all through the night. Even though my household was dysfunctional my grandmother made me go to church. St. James Baptist Church is the church I grew up in and one of the Deacons taught me and my cousins in Sunday school. He was one of a few positive male role models in my life at that time. Deacon Morris and his brother Pastor Morris taught me that Jesus loves me just as I was and they taught me the foundation of Christ. Throughout elementary and junior high school I continued to go to church when I was 13 I gave my life to Jesus and got baptized. I had an understanding of what my Christian life was supposed to be but really didn't know how to live it. I didn't have anyone in my home as a true "Christian" example.

My dad would come to visit me and I knew how to find him if I wanted to. Dad always had nice cars and nice things and then all of a sudden he didn't. He became a drug addict and an alcoholic. He made a lot of broken promises to me but he also tried to be around even though it wasn't everything I needed from him as a father. By the time my mom came back to live in Emporia in the summer of 1986 I was 14 years old and thought I was grown even though I wanted to be with my mom I had a lot of resentment towards her. We stayed in an extended stay hotel for a while then with my grandmother but not for long because mom and grandma argued about everything. When we got our place I thought I was grown and was not trying to listen to anything my mom had to say to me because she did not raise me. I can look at it now and see I was very angry and rebellious I saw her more as a sister than a mother. Moving in with my mother changed my life. I got freedom from my strict grandmother who by this time was sober. I also met my high school sweetheart Richard that summer. After falling head over hills in love with Richard I gave him my virginity (or at least what was left of it) a year or so later. Richard and I went to my mother and he told her that we were having sex and we wanted to get on the pill. I don't remember ever having anyone tell me that I shouldn't have sex before marriage not saying that would have stopped me but who knows. This may sound crazy but having sex on my own free will was freeing to me in a sense. I felt like I took back control over my own body that had been used and abused by my uncle for so those years when I was younger. I found my voice but my voice was full of anger and pain and I didn't care who I hurt with my words. I would say whatever came to mind. That old saying "Hurt people, hurt people" is so very true. That's why now when I see a person that seems to be mean and act ugly I wonder what happened in their life that made them that way. There's some painful story behind that anger that person is carrying and has probably been carrying for a long time and they don't feel like they can trust anyone with it. Don't be so quick to judge them or retaliate against them. Pray for them and love the hell out of them through the love of God.

Let's Pray:

Father in the name of Jesus I ask that You would place powerful praying women in the life of this Princess to help her learn how to trust again. Help her to trust You and herself first. Show her that even though she made mistakes that the mistakes don't make her. Show her that the things that have been done to her don't define who she is now. Help her to see herself as victorious not a victim. Lord, show her freedom in You not in using her body to get what she wants but giving her body to You Father as a living sacrifice holy and acceptable unto You in Jesus name, Amen.

Do you know anyone that seems to be angry all the time or mean spirited? Is that person you? Write a prayer for healing, peace, and restoration for that person.

_____

_____

_____

_____

_____

_____

_____

_____

_____

_____

_____

_____

_____

My life with mom was far from strict. She was still partying and would bring home different men all the time. There were even a couple of different white men who tried to seduce me one I had to fight off but I never told my mom or anyone else about the incident. Mom had no discrimination when it came to men she loved them all. She was very social, she never met a stranger and when she walked into a room her personality took over the place. She was always the life of the party and this was very embarrassing for me as a teenager. A couple of times after she had been out partying she came home and tried to cook herself something to eat. She was drunk and or high and ended up passing out leaving the food to burn. The smell woke me up to a house filled with thick black smoke. Both times this happened I dragged her outside and crawled back into the house to turn off the stove and open the windows. By the time I got back outside she would be waking up yelling at me and trying to fight me because she didn't realize that she almost killed us. One of those times Richard had spent the night with me and seen it firsthand.

Let's Pray:

Lord, we ask You to cover every child that is living with a parent or guardian that is an addict of any kind. Encamp Your heavenly angels all around that child to keep them protected and safe. Place a loving, kind, mature adult in that child's life that will help them be safe and help the parent to get the help they need to live a clean productive life. Help the children to know they have a purpose and a destiny in You and help them to pursue it. We pray they will choose a different lifestyle then what they are seeing every day at home in Jesus' name I pray, Amen.

Do you know any addicts? List them and their children and write a prayer for them.

_____

_____

_____

_____

_____

_____

_____

_____

_____

_____

_____

_____

_____

_____

_____

_____

At the age of 14 Marquita and I also got our first jobs working for McDonald's. At this time my mom started charging me rent and making me buy my own clothes. When I went to the bank to deposit my first check I found out that my mother had taken all my money out of my account that I had saved from birthdays and the money I used to find (once when me and grandma were walking downtown I found $300) and put in my account over the years. When I confronted her about it she said she needed it to pay bills and would pay it back. During my sophomore year of high school I was depressed and didn't know it. I felt like a complete failure about everything, I had quit my McDonald's job and applied for a different job and didn't get hired. Richard and I were having issues; my mom was doing her own thing and didn't recognize my issues. I felt I had no one to talk to so I decided to kill myself. I took a bunch of Tylenol but all it did was made me very nauseous. Not dying really made me feel like a failure, I felt like I couldn't even kill myself right! At that time I decided not to try it again. (God had a plan for me) I never told anyone until a few years ago that I tried to commit suicide, I guess I was ashamed. By the time I was a junior in high school I was tired of my mom's lifestyle and I was paying bills anyway so Richard and I got an apartment together. I was 16 years old and he was 18, my mom had to sign consent forms for me because I was a minor but he and I paid the bills.

Richard and I living together only lasted about 5 months. Before long we broke up and I was back living with my mom. After moving back in with mom I got a little wild. I started going to Ft. Riley army base with my cousins and friends to party at the clubs. I would use my older cousin's I.D. to get into the clubs. I was drinking alcohol more and not valuing my own body as much as I should have. I knew I was cute and had a nice figure but didn't know my worth. I felt a freedom I hadn't felt before, and I gave away my cookie far too easily. I didn't have anyone in my life to tell me to value my body and everyone else around me was doing it too so I thought it was all right. Of course, back then I didn't realize that the sexual abuse that happened to me when I was younger was a mental trauma and the way I dealt with it was sexually acting out being promiscuous. I needed counseling but that was unheard of in my black family back then.

Let's Pray:

Father in the mighty name of Jesus I ask You, Lord, to heal the issues of the heart of the Princess reading this prayer. Lord, where her parents may have not known how to love her the way she needed them to love her bring healing to that empty place within her that is still seeking a mother's love and or a father's love. Father, I bind up the spirit of suicide. I declare and decree that Your Princess will live and not die to declare the good works of the Lord.

Touch Your daughter to know that she is not a failure and that You have an assignment for her to complete. Help her to see herself the way You see her God that she is above and not beneath. Help her to see that no matter what anyone else says about her that she is valued and valuable to Your Kingdom. Show her the value in keeping her virginity until she is married and keeping her temple holy for You Lord. Father, show Your daughter the counselor that she needs to see to help her talk about her past and help her through her process of healing. Give Your Princess peace and take away all shame of seeking a therapist because You send people to help us. Lord, You see the trouble of those who need You and You consider their grief and help them. Thank You, Father, for comforting Your daughter and making her whole in You because You are a good, good Father in Jesus' name, Amen.

What are the issues of your heart? What troubles you that you need God to heal? Write a prayer asking God to heal those issues and at the end of the prayer praise and thank God for your healing.

_____

_____

_____

_____

_____

_____

_____

_____

_____

_____

_____

_____

_____

1990-1995

The sad truth is that my main goals while in high school were to not get pregnant and to graduate on time. Understand getting pregnant in high school was something that has happened for generations in my family and is still happening and not graduating high school is another one but I wasn't going to let that be part of my story. One evening during my senior year of high school my Aunt Phyllis brought her new boyfriend over to my mom's house along with his friend both of them were soldiers stationed at Ft. Riley. The friend and I hit it off and began dating; he was 11 years older than me and already had several children (Yep that's my daddy issues popping up again). He discharged out of the army and moved back to Ohio. We still tried to date long distance and I went to visit him in Toledo on my spring break but it was too much distance to keep it going and he was a different person around his family.

There was a couple that had moved next door to my mom's house during my senior year of high school. They had been working at the beef plant for several months to save up money to move back to Tulsa. I had gone with them to Tulsa to visit a couple of times while they were living in Emporia and loved it. They asked me if I wanted to go with them when they moved back and me looking for a way out of Emporia said yes. Three days after graduating high school I moved to

Tulsa, Oklahoma. I thought I was having the time of my life there, partying and doing whatever I wanted to or thought I was grown enough to do. I was in Tulsa for about three months; while there I got involved with an abusive man. Of course, he started off being a very charming sweet person that showered me with attention and he was very good looking. He would always say to me "If you love someone let them go and if they don't come back to you hunt them down and kill them." At first, I thought it was funny but the more I got to know him I knew he meant it. He would backhand me in the face while he was driving down the street if I had done something that set him off. I will never forget one night after I had broken up with him because

I couldn't take the abuse anymore he was driving around looking for me. I had been hiding at a friend's house when he stopped at the house asking for me. They told him I wasn't there but he continued driving by the house. I knew what kind of craziness he would do to that friend and his family so I left the house because I didn't want anyone to get hurt. I made it to the inside of the corner store and that's where he found me. I told the gas station clerk to call the police but the ex-boyfriend told him that if he did he would come back and kill him. He dragged me into the car which his cousin was driving and he made me sit in the middle of them so I couldn't get out of the car. By that time my best friend at the time showed up in the parking lot and got in the car (I don't know why she didn't stay away and just call the police). We drove around Tulsa most of the night; he was driving very erratically, on the wrong side of the street into oncoming traffic. A Police helicopter was flying around. At one point he had let me get in the back seat of the car. My friend and I were able to jump out of the car when he slowed down enough at a stop sign. We ran and hid but he found me and took me to drop his cousin off. Then he took me out in the country on this long dark road and told me I could either get beat or I could find my way back home. I took off jogging down the high way and he drove off. As I got over a hill he was sitting on the trunk of his car laughing at me, telling me to get in the car. I told him no and kept jogging, he made me get in the car and all I could think is this man is going to kill me if I don't play along and make him feel that I wanted to stay with him. So that's what I did I told him I didn't want to break up but I needed to go home because I had to go to work in the morning and it was late. He took me home and as I was slamming the door shut I screamed F-You and ran in the house. The next morning he got into the house and came into the bathroom while I was taking a shower getting ready for work (scared the crap out of me). He was saying he was sorry and wanted to drive me to work, by this time I knew the only way to get away from him was to leave the state and not tell anyone where I was going. Instead of going back to Emporia, I went from one bad situation into another. I had been talking to my ex-boyfriend that lives in Ohio on the phone he never told me that he was living with another woman and she was pregnant with his baby. I didn't find out about any of that until I was in Toledo. He ended up being an abusive cheater too. The difference with him is that I fought back. I would freeze 2-liter pop bottles with water and beat him with them I also cut him with a piece of glass sending him to the hospital. My last straw with him was shortly after finding out I was pregnant at the age of 19, we fought, and he choked me until I went unconscious. That night I planned on killing him but thank God he woke up with me standing over him with a knife. The next day I called home and told my mom and grandma that I was pregnant and needed to come home because one of us was going to end up dead and the other in prison.

Let's Prayer:

Father in the mighty name of Jesus I come asking You to deliver all of Your Princesses out of abusive relationships. Lord You did not create Your children to be beaten, bruised, assaulted, or damaged by anyone. Give Your Princess strength and a way of escape to get out of that toxic situation and into a safe place. Place people in her path that will help her and not judge her. Father, cover her with Your feathers and give her refuge under Your wings. Thank You Lord that Your faithfulness is her shield and armor in Jesus' name, Amen.

Are you in an abusive relationship or know someone who is, whether it is physical, emotional, or verbal? Write a prayer for that person asking God for a way of escape, wisdom, insight, and people to help them get out safely and for protection.

_____

_____

_____

_____

_____

_____

_____

_____

_____

_____

_____

_____

My mom and grandmother sent me a bus ticket and I moved back to Kansas and in with my mom. I started attending the church I grew up in again and became a Sunday school teacher for a short time. I thank God that the people in the church were not judgmental toward me being unmarried and pregnant in the church. Linda, Angel and I got an apartment together we were all pregnant and single (example of one of our family's generational curses). We also spent a lot of time with my cousin Sharon who was like a big sister to me. We loved to just hang out talk, cook, eat and laugh together. Sharon gave us so much great advice on everything from men to cooking. I had my first son in September of 1991 his name is

Christian. About a year after he was born I enrolled into college at Emporia State University majoring in sociology and minoring in psychology. While I attended ESU I went to one of the school counselors. I knew I needed help dealing with my childhood abandonment, rejection, and abuse issues. I remember I had 2 or 3 sessions with the counselor and she told me that I needed to find another counselor because I wouldn't cry. Needless to say I didn't go back to a counselor for many years. I only attended ESU for a year it got to be too much for me at that time. Christian started having what the doctor called "fainting spells" right after his 1st birthday. His eyes would roll back in his head, his lips and nose would turn blue, and his breathing would become shallow. I would rush him to the hospital or call an ambulance but by the time help came he would be sleeping. I felt like the doctors didn't believe me until one day he did it while we were in the Emergency Room and I had medical witnesses. Christian had stopped saying the few words he had been saying. I took him to neurologists and other doctors who ran several tests on him and told me that there was nothing wrong with his brain that they could see that would cause him not to speak anymore. The doctors put him on medication for seizures. I beat myself up a lot of years feeling like I did something wrong that made Christian "retarded" is what the doctors labeled him but I say he is "special needs."

When people ask me what his disability is I tell them he is just Christian there is no other way to describe him.

Let's Pray:

Father in the name of Jesus I come to You asking You to give every mother who has a special needs child the right people in her corner that will help her and support her to be able to take care of her baby. Lord, help this mother to know that she is a special kind of person that is equipped with a special kind of love to nurture and raise this special gift. Give her the strength, endurance, and power to advocate for her child to get the best care, treatments, and education. Lord I also pray for healing for the child from the top of his/her head to the sole of its feet. I thank You that the child will grow up confident and knowing that he/she is fearfully and wonderfully made in Jesus' name, Amen.

Do you know someone with a special needs child or do you have a special needs child? Write a prayer lifting that child and parent up to the Lord.

_____

_____

_____

_____

_____

_____

_____

_____

_____

_____

_____

_____

_____

_____

_____

_____

I had met and started dating another soldier who had moved Christian and me to Manhattan, KS. I was able to get him into a good program to get help with his delays. Christian didn't say another word until I was walking him to school one morning and he said "bird" and pointed at a bird, he was 2 years old. I cried like a baby. We eventually moved to Junction City and my sister-cousin Linda and her son Devante who is the same age as Christian came to live with us. Linda is the one who encouraged me to go back to school. We babysat each other's son while we both attended Brown Mackie College I studied court reporting and secretarial training, did that for a couple of years not graduating either program. I didn't know my purpose and didn't know how to figure it out. I had my second son Davian in July of 1995. His father Damian and I dated for a few years. He was good with Christian and Davian but couldn't seem to get motivated to help me to provide for the family. He smoked way too much weed and he didn't want to grow up so we were off and on for a couple of years. I didn't want to be a single mother of 2 sons by 2 different men and not be married to either one of them, but I refused to settle for foolishness.

Let's Pray:

Father in the name of Jesus I lift up the Princess reading this book and ask You, Lord, to help her to know her worth. Show her that she does not have to settle for a piece of a man because You have the perfect man for her if she waits on You. Help her to know that even if she isn't married to her baby's daddy doesn't mean another man won't marry her and love her. Lord touch the man that You have for her and help him to see her the way You see her and love her children as if they were his own. Don't let him miss out on his good thing and obtaining favor from You because she is a single mother. Lord, I thank You for covering this Princess with Your glory in Jesus' name, Amen.

What are some goals you want to accomplish to better yourself? List them and the write a prayer asking the Holy Spirit to help you accomplish them.

_____

_____

_____

_____

_____

_____

_____

_____

_____

_____

_____

_____

_____

_____

_____

_____

_____

1995-1997

Linda moved to Texas to live with our other sister-cousin Angel and after Linda left, I eventually dropped out of Brown Mackie. I ended up moving back to Manhattan and attended Crum's Beauty College to get my certification to do nails (it was only a 3-month program and I knew I needed to finish something to get a job to get off welfare). Right before I graduated I was hired in Junction City at The Mane Thing Beauty Salon so my boys and I moved once again back to Junction City. I loved doing nails because it gave me a chance to listen to people's stories and to share some of my own. On Monday, Dec. 30th, 1996 I hadn't been at work very long when I received a telephone call from Marquita telling me that my mom had died. I thought she was playing some sick joke on me and I hung up the phone after saying some choice word to her but right after I hung up Aunt Terri Ann called me and told me that it was true and that I needed to get home as soon as possible. I don't remember fainting but I remember coming to and people being all around me asking me if I was all right. My coworkers called Damian (this was during our on-again times) to let him know what happened and he drove me and my sons the hour and a half drive to Emporia. I thought so many things during that time like how I had just seen my mother at Christmas and how I almost didn't go home because my car was so raggedy. I also remembered the last words she said to me. She told me that my boys were bad and that she loved me but I didn't say it back to her. I was angry at myself for not saying it back to her because now she'll never hear it again. I love you was something I hardly ever said to her but if I knew that would be the last time I would ever see her I would have said that and so much more. I thought about how my mom was only 39 years old and I was 24 and she had only been back in my life full time for 10 years! When I arrived at my grandma's house in Emporia all of my family was there and I still couldn't believe that she was dead so I asked my family to tell me what happen I wanted every little detail. I begged my uncle and cousins to take me to the site where the car wrecked. When we arrived at the crash site I could see some of my mom's belongings on the ground. I picked my mother's hair up off the ground and some of her belongings that had fallen out of her purse. It was in a horse field. I couldn't believe my mother died on a winter night in a horse field in a car all by herself. I then asked them to take me to the garage where the car she was in was being stored. When we arrived at the garage I saw the car and it looked like a smashed can. I was told that the driver of the car and my mother had been our partying and had alcohol and drugs in their systems. The driver was going about 130 mph when he missed the curve and hit the ditch making the car do flips from front to trunk, flipping about 8 times. I started pulling my mother's hair off the passenger's side of the car looking at her blood that had dried on it made me very angry. I never knew I could feel so much hate toward someone. I wanted my family to take me to the hospital I needed to see what he looked like. I wanted to kill him but more than anything I wanted to see his face, but they wouldn't take me to the hospital. I couldn't believe that when he came to he made his way to a house where he got help but when he was asked if there was anyone with him he said no. It wasn't until the police went to the car that they discovered my mother was in the car dead. I don't know if she would still be alive if she would have gotten help sooner but the fact that he said he was alone infuriated me. The coroner told me that she died instantly but I knew he was only saying that to try to give me some peace. I read his report and seen that there were fluids in her lungs that wouldn't have been there if she had died instantly. My Uncle Bob told me that her facial expression looked like she had been crying and that there was still white paint on her face that they couldn't cover up or get off her from the car. Over the next year or so while the man was waiting for his trial to start was arrested two more times for drunk driving. His lawyer had the nerve to call me and ask me not to protest him getting probation. I couldn't believe it; this man wanted me to let the man that killed my mother walk free! I lost it! I don't remember everything I said but I do remember this much of it. I was yelling at him "my mom is just another dead nigga off the streets to you". The man my mom was with that night is a white man it infuriated me and I felt that he didn't value my mother's life. This was just more fuel added to all the anger and hurt from my life that I didn't know what to do with or how to let it go.

Let's Pray:

Lord I ask You to give Your Princess peace that passes all understanding with all traumatic things that have happened in her life. She doesn't understand why these things have

*happened and may never get the
answers she's looking to get help her
to be at peace. Lord where anger and
confusion have set in I bind it up right
now because You Father are not the
author of confusion. God give her
clarity! Help her to not feel like she's
alone so please comfort her Lord.
Father, give her rest; help her to be
able to sleep peacefully at night. Send
Your heavenly angels to minister to
her right now and even when she
sleeps speak to her. Thank You,
Father, that depression and bitterness
will not set into her life because You
are God of her life in Jesus' name,
Amen.*

Have you lost a loved one due to someone else's neglect or carelessness? Write a prayer asking God to help you heal and forgive or write a letter to your loved one saying what you wish you would have told them before they died.

_____

_____

_____

_____

_____

_____

_____

_____

_____

_____

_____

_____

_____

Grandma and I decided to cremate her because that's what mom wanted. I remembered a conversation we once had when she told me that she wanted to be cremated and her ashes to be thrown over New York. I did go out and purchase her clothes for the wake. I remember the funeral home director telling me to make sure I bought a turban or scarf for her head (she had a lot of head trauma). I did go to her wake but I didn't go see her body because I wanted to remember her the way I had last seen her on Christmas. After her funeral my lawyer called me and told me that I needed to come to his office to sign paperwork for the settlement with the insurance company for the death of my mom. I asked the lawyer if he had the police photos from the wreck, he said yes. I told him I wanted to see them when I came to the office. The night before I was to go to the lawyer's office I had a dream and in that dream I saw the wreck site with my mother scalped, lying dead with half of her body under the car. When I arrived to the lawyer's office, he gave me the pictures of the crash scene and everything I saw in my dream was exactly what the pictures showed. I couldn't believe that God had shown me everything the night before so when I saw the pictures I wouldn't be shocked. Around this time I began to have migraine headaches. I wanted to hire someone to kidnap him and take him to a shed in the woods where I could go beat and torture him whenever I felt like it. I had so much hate for this man it was affecting me physically and I didn't even know it. Not long after my mom died I was visiting my dad and my little brother Tony Jr. was there and I asked my dad why his mom treated me the way she did (she stopped being involved with me when I was in high school). My dad told me "well she doesn't think that you are my biological child but I have always thought you were and I love you no matter what." I was absolutely stunned! I had not heard this before and I was mad because now my mom is dead and I couldn't question her about it.

Let's Pray:

Father in the name of Jesus I come to You asking You to help Your Princess know the truth of her life. Reveal to her who she is in You. Help her Lord to let go of the pain and uncertainty from her parents and help her to know that she has a Heavenly Father that has adopted her and will use her because of her story. Lord reveal to her every buried disappointment, hurt, and anger that is causing her health issues. Help her to recognize them and release them to You Father in Jesus' name, Amen.

Are you having frequent migraines, high blood pressure, cancer, or another illness that maybe caused by un-forgiveness in your life? Write a prayer asking God to reveal the root of your disease and release to Him.

_____

_____

_____

_____

_____

_____

_____

_____

_____

_____

_____

3 months and 1 day after my mom died I was preparing to go to work when I received another telephone call on the Monday after Easter telling me that my grandmother, the woman that raised me had died at home in her sleep due to complications of diabetes. I had just left there the evening before because I went to visit her for Easter. I seem to have taken my grandmothers death harder than my mother's. Now looking back at it I believe I was still in a bit of shock from mom's death and then the fact I lost 2 mothers in 3 months was something I can't even put words to the emotions I was feeling. I was a person that went to clubs, drank and smoked weed but after the loss of my mom and grandmother I smoked a lot more often. It helped me to sleep and

eat not knowing that I was using it to self- medicate because I was grief stricken and depressed. I don't remember if anyone told me to go to counseling but I'm sure if they did, I probably told them that I was all right.

Let's Pray:

Lord thank You for being a healer. I ask that You continue to heal the pain of Your Princesses that may have lots her mother. Father, help her to see that in life there is a season for everything and help her to also know that You God make no mistakes. Her heart is broken right now and she needs You to give her strength to hold on to You Lord. Father, she needs Your Holy Spirit to comfort her right now and give her Your peace that passes all understanding in Jesus' name, Amen.

What area do you need God to strengthen in? Are still processing a death of a loved one, pet, job? Write a prayer asking God for strength to endure the process.

_____

_____

_____

_____

_____

_____

_____

_____

_____

_____

_____

_____

_____

One of my mother's friends had promised my grandmother before she died that she would keep an eye on me and my boys. About 2 months after grandma died Tela came to visit me in Junction City; we went to a hole in the wall called the Sugar Shack for a few drinks. I went to the restroom and when I walked out I saw a beautiful tall dark chocolate man standing at the pool table. He asked me if I wanted to play and I said sure I'll beat you real quick. He smiled and we played pool and talked. By the end of the night through my tipsiness I told Tela that I was going to marry him. Alvin and I drove to Florida Memorial Day weekend before we got married so that I could meet his family. Everyone was very nice to me but of course there were comments made to my husband about me having 2 sons already. Some of the women and one of his uncles "warned" him about me. He didn't listen and a couple of weeks later Alvin and I got married on June 11, 1997 in the Junction City Court House. I would not encourage anyone to do what we did. We were two very broken people at the time that didn't think or talk about the truth of our issues and baggage we brought into the marriage. Alvin was also raised by his grandparents and suffered from the same rejection, abandonment, low self-esteem and fear of being alone issues I did. Also right after we got married I got custody of my little cousin who was 13 years old at the time and I found out I was pregnant. Now Alvin and I had discussed having a baby after we got married because he didn't have any biological children and decided I would stop taking the pill. I knew I would be pregnant within the month because I am very fertile. So the next month when I told Alvin I was pregnant and he said to me "Congratulations" I didn't know how to react to that reaction (to this day I still give him a hard time about it). Alvin's family accepted all of the children as their own even my little cousin. Even though my mother in love (law) didn't seem to like me very much she still treated the children as her own grandchildren.

My husband was in the Army so we had a few choices for the next duty station, one being Germany. It's crazy because when I heard that my first thought was heck no I don't know him like that, he's not getting me halfway around the world away from my family and I can't just get in a car and drive home if he acts a fool but yet I had married him. So we were stationed in Ft. Stewart Georgia.

1998-2003

After being in Georgia for about 7 months our third son Isaiah was born in April of 1998. While living in Ft. Stewart, I had to travel back to Kansas for the trial of the man that was driving the car when my mother died. He was sentenced to 7 years for vehicular manslaughter and I spoke at the sentencing because I was considered the victim. I despised him and it affected my entire life. I had written a statement to read but was so angry and emotional I didn't read it I just started yelling at him telling him about how much I hated him.

Let's Pray:

Father in the name of Jesus I come to You lifting up any Princess that will have to make a victim's statement or any statement that she has to make that will make an impact on those who hear it. Help her Lord to keep her composure and to say everything she needs to say. Give her the words to express her loss, anger, and sadness. Lord, give her the strength to persevere and stand knowing that You are with her in Jesus' name, Amen.

What has happened that you need to make a statement about? Pray asking God for the words then begin to write.

_____

_____

_____

_____

_____

_____

_____

_____

_____

_____

_____

_____

_____

_____

_____

Our marriage was a train wreck waiting to happen and having my teenage cousin brought more dysfunction to an already hard situation. She had her own set of issues that at the time I wasn't equipped to help her. After being in Georgia for a couple of years it happens my husband and I separated and after my cousin continued to run away from home and do other things I had to sign her over to the state. She was 15 when she went into the foster care system. It broke my heart but I knew it was something I had to do. She ended up in a home with an older black lady that loved the Lord. This was probably one of the best things for her because we were not mature enough to help her.

Alvin had a drinking problem and he also had a problem being a married man, he liked the attention of many women. There was no way our marriage was going to work without help. We weren't saved nor were we trying to be at that time. I had always told him that cheating would be one of the things that were grounds for divorce in our marriage. I left my husband after finding out about the affairs. I was so hurt from my past relationships and the abuse I endured from the men in my life that having my husband do this to me was not a surprise to me but it did hurt me because I had taken my marriage vows seriously and stayed faithful to him. I don't know that premarital counseling would have helped us but I do think it is something every couple should have just so they can know what the other person thinks about what a marriage should be.

Alvin had to move into the barracks and his roommate was a young man named Bennett and he was on fire for the Lord. He had Bible studies with my husband and taught him how to fast and pray. Alvin accepted Jesus while living in the barracks and found a church that he got involved in. During this time Davian was already visiting his father Damian so I asked him if he could stay with him a little longer while we went through all of the drama we were dealing with. I moved everything out of housing and into a storage unit while Alvin was out in the field for work. The boys and I moved with a friend of mine but someone called the Dept. of Children and Family Services and they came to the house investigating. It was like all hell broke loose in my life and I had no one I could trust because she told me that I needed to get out of her house because she didn't want any trouble. I understood and the boys and I went to a women's shelter who helped me get my place for me and my 3 sons. I remember during this time Alvin had the boys for a visit and his mother and aunts had come to town to check on him. They had taken Alvin and the boys out to eat and I had already told Alvin that the boys needed to be clean when he returned them to me because we had to meet with the social worker. Well, when I picked the boys up

Isaiah's shirt was filthy because he didn't have a bib on when he ate lunch and I went off on Alvin. He said he had told his family that I was going to be upset but they didn't think I was going to be as mad as I was for a dirty shirt. But to me, it was so much more than that I was a scared mother that was all alone away from my family in the middle of a battle with my husband, the military, and with DFC! My main focus was not losing my children because of my husband's foolishness and alcoholism.

Let's Pray:

Father in the name of Jesus I lift up every Princess that will ever be put in a situation where she feels all alone with the world against her. Help her know that You are with her and that You are fighting the battle for her even though it doesn't look like it or feel like it. Help her feel at peace that her children will not be taken from her. Show her who is for her and who You have sent to help her through this wilderness time of her life. Thank You Lord that You will give her the right attitude to go through the storm and give her favor with those she feels is against her. I thank You Lord for Your glory shining through the dark clouds that are hovering in her life right now and help her to remember that trouble doesn't last always in Jesus' name, Amen.

Have you been in a situation that you felt alone? Do you know another woman that is going through a hard time right now? Write a prayer for that woman for strength, peace, finances and whatever else God puts on your heart.

_____

_____

_____

_____

_____

_____

_____

_____

_____

_____

_____

I started dating someone that I had worked with at my previous job after I started working at Walmart in Hinesville. He helped me with the boys and would take them to Alvin and pick them up from him sometimes for me (yes I wanted Alvin to hurt the way I hurt from his cheating).

During the separation, Alvin and I would meet in public places to hand off the children to each other. We had both said some crazy stuff to each other and I didn't trust him at the time to not be violent with me even though we only had one physical encounter before where we were arguing and he grazed my cheek enough to set me off and I jumped on his back when he was trying to run away from me he never hit me but I didn't want him to ever think he could. After a while, I started seeing changes in Alvin but I didn't quite trust that it was real. When he asked me if I would start coming to church with him I thought well if he has truly changed I don't want another woman to reap the benefits of all the hell I had been through so I went to church with him. The second time I came to church with him I received Jesus as my Lord and Savior and three days later I didn't smoke cigarettes or weed any longer and my life change drastically I even stopped cursing. Alvin and I got back together and I joined Live Oak Church of God (LOC) in October of 1999 and one of the first things Alvin talked to me about was tithing. Alvin told me that Pastor Mike Cowart had taught on tithing and that we are to return the tithe to God cheerfully. I had reservations about giving my money to some preacher but after Alvin explained that we weren't giving it to the preacher we were returning to God what is His and whatever the church does with it after that is between them and God. I wanted to please God and be in right standing with Him so I agreed to test God with my tithe along with my husband.

Let's Pray:

Father, I pray that this Princess accepts You wholeheartedly and that she trusts You to be the head of her life and relationships. Touch her husband that they would agree in tithing. Teach them how to trust You with their tithe that You would bring increase into their lives through the obedience of tithing. Fill the home and marriage with a peace that they have never felt before and help them to walk together in agreeance with You. Father, place Holy Spirit- filled people in both the lives of the Princess and her husband, that will pray with them and give them godly counsel when issues arise in their household. Thank You Lord for their peaceful home and the heavenly angels You have placed around it to protect it in Jesus' name, Amen.

Do you tithe? If not why don't you trust God with a dime of every dollar? Write a prayer asking God to help you trust Him and to give you the courage to test Him with the tithe. If you do tithe write a prayer for a person that you know doesn't tithe yet.

_____

_____

_____

_____

_____

_____

_____

_____

_____

_____

_____

_____

Alvin and I renewed our vows Dec.31st, 1999 in church with our sons and Associate Pastor Todd after being separated for six months. We knew we needed to repent and get our past covered under the Blood of Jesus. After I got saved the Lord kept dealing with me about forgiving Mearl but I wasn't ready to let the anger go that I had for him. That sounds so crazy to me now that I am saying it but it is the truth. Hate is truly a cancer that eats away at you daily and a lot of the time you don't even know that's what is making you sick.   We attended LOC for a couple of years and while at LOC I met a minister named Sister Katrina who was and still is a mighty prayer warrior. She taught me how to pray and seek the Holy Spirit. There I learned how to hear the voice of God and know who I am in Him. I met her at the church for 5am prayer for as long as I could. Also while working at Wal-Mart I met Sheila, Vernell, and Carmen these 3 women were absolutely God sent. We all worked at Wal-Mart and began praying together at work, at each other's homes, at each other's churches and wherever else we could. We saw God move quickly when we prayed, it was amazing! There were even times we smelt the fragrance of roses after we prayed. My faith in God grew tremendously when God connected me with these 3 prayer warriors.

Let's Pray:

Father in the name of Jesus I pray that You would provide divine intervention for this Princess that she would cross paths with the person that is to be her prayer partner. I ask You to take them deeper in prayer that they would touch heaven and have a God encounter. Holy Spirit, teach them how to pray, give them the words to pray and help to push their way into Your presence. Father, cover them that they not be distracted from prayer and keep their relationship covered in the blood of Jesus to protect them from the plots and schemes of the enemy that will try to keep them from praying together in Jesus' name, Amen.

Do you have a prayer partner? If not write a prayer for God to connect you with someone but if you do have a prayer partner write a prayer covering your relationship.

_____

_____

_____

_____

_____

_____

_____

_____

_____

_____

_____

_____

_____

I gave birth to our baby boy Ezekiel in August of 2001. Eventually my husband got out of the army and started a civilian job as a manager at a fast food restaurant. During this time we struggled more financially and I remember one day the water pressure changed in the house as I was doing dishes, everyone took their showers, I washed clothes etc. I thought oh the city must be working on the water lines in the neighborhood again. We had not paid the water bill because we just didn't have the money but that day I went to pay the bill. When I arrived to the water department and paid the bill the lady told me that someone would be out to turn my water on as soon as possible. I looked at her and said ma'am my water is not off. She said

Mrs. Isaac your water has been off for 7 days. I looked at her and said no it hasn't I explained to her how the entire family took showers, how I ran the dish washer and washing machine and told her everything else we had done within that 7 days. She insisted that our water had been disconnected! I heard the Lord speak to me and say "Your well will never run dry". I started praising God and I called Alvin and told him we were both in awe of God. When I got home the first thing I did was turned on the water in the kitchen and nothing came out. Not a drop! I went to the bathroom and tried the sink then the bath tub and not a drop came out of them either! I was so excited and I knew that testing God with the tithe was something we would always do.

Let's Pray:

Father in the name of Jesus I ask You to help this Princess to trust You with her life including her finances. Lord where she has been skeptical in tithing I pray that You would give her the faith in You to test You and try You to see that You are faithful and true to Your word. Lord as she tests You and tithes and gives I pray that she will see clearly how You make every end meet. Thank You Lord for her overflow that You provide her with to be able to sow more seed and help others in Jesus name, Amen.

Yes I know we just prayed about tithing on a previous page but tithing has been very important in my life. God has blessed me and my family and I know it's because of our faithfulness to tithing. It's about being obedient to God's word and having faith in Him.

Is there anything still keeping you from trusting God with your tithe? If so write another prayer asking the Lord to help you trust Him. If you already are tithing write a prayer for someone else to see God move in their finances by them testing Him with their tithe.

_____

_____

_____

_____

_____

_____

_____

_____

_____

_____

Alvin moved from job to job and he also went to Baltimore to stay with his Aunt Teresa and started working at a restaurant thinking that was going to be our next move. But one day I was praying and I heard the Lord say to tell Alvin to come home because we were supposed to move to Florida back to Alvin's home town. I immediately called Alvin and told him what the Lord said and not even a week later he came home and applied to some state positions in Florida. He was hired and we moved to his home town Gretna, Florida where it rained the first 40 days and nights we were there, I cried and gained weight not realizing that I was depressed. Alvin had gotten a job at the state hospital and I was at home with the children. We had gotten them into school and I was very unhappy about the schools and teachers there. When Alvin and I had went to meet Isaiah's head start teacher she said "testses" instead of tests. I looked at my husband and he looked at me like please don't say anything cause he knew what I was thinking. When we left I told him that if Isaiah came home talking like her I was going to have a talk with the principal.

Around this time God started dealing with my heart about forgiving the man that was driving the car when my mom died. I didn't want to but I knew I couldn't do what God had called me to do with hate in my heart towards him. The Lord instructed me to write Mearl a letter and to tell him whatever I needed to say to get it out but at the end of the letter I had to tell him that I forgave him. It was up to me whether or not I mailed it to him, burned it, keep it or tear it up. I chose to mail it to him along with pictures of my mom and pictures of me and my family. I felt such a release off of me when I did this. I didn't know if he would reply to it or not but I had to do this so I could work towards closure.

Let's Pray:

Father in the name of Jesus I ask You to touch Your daughter. Lord bring back to her remembrance those people and circumstances that she has suppressed and help her to write the letters she needs to write to all the people in her past that have hurt, used, and abused her. Lord show her who is currently in her life that she

*needs to write a goodbye letter to so
she can move forward in Your peace
and forgiveness. Help her Father to let
go of the pain and the people even if
she never gets the apology she
deserves. Lord even if she needs to
forgive herself and help her to do so
quickly. Help her to know that the
forgiveness she gives to others is so
she can be free to live her life to the
fullest in Jesus' name, Amen.*

Is there someone that has hurt you that you need to forgive or is there someone in your life you need to let go of. Even if it's fear, guilt, shame, write a letter letting go and forgiving.

_____

_____

_____

_____

_____

_____

_____

_____

_____

_____

_____

_____

_____

After Ezekiel turned 2 years old Alvin and I decided it was time for me to get a job so I began working at Goodwill in Tallahassee as an assistant manager. While there I met a woman that became my prayer partner and we began a 501 c3 nonprofit that fed the homeless in the area. Alvin was depressed too and started drinking when we moved back to his home town. He had always told me that he never wanted to live there again and I understood that feeling because I never want to live in my hometown again either. But when God tells you to do something it's best to do it. After a few months Alvin lost his job at the state mental hospital and his drinking got bad again. I was angry that he reverted back to his old ways of dealing with problems. He started staying out late and coming home drunk. I felt so disrespected by him because he knew how my mother died and here he was drinking and driving. We were living in an old trailer that was at least 30 years old, it had holes in the closet floor where an opossum came through the floor looking at the boys and Alvin one night and any time we took a shower a frog or lizard might be in the tub looking at us. We eventually moved into my husband's grandparent's old house next to the trailer. I began working at the state mental hospital the 11pm to 7am shift. It was a very interesting job and it seemed to me that the people working there were crazier than the patients. Not long after I began working for the mental hospital is when I received a letter from Mearl it had been about a year later and he was still in prison. My reaction of receiving the letter surprised me I cried uncontrollably just holding the letter in my hands. When I opened the letter and read the words "I'm so sorry. I loved your mother. I wish it was me that died" my heart hurt for him and I reached out to him through more letters throughout the seven years he was in prison. When he was released from prison we talked on the phone and continue to talk on the phone at least twice a year. He was very remorseful and always apologizing for what happened. I was constantly encouraging him to let it go and figure out what his purpose was in life.

In 2003 my little cousin Eddie came to live with us in Florida from Kansas. His mother my little cousin and Marquita's little sister had died a couple of years before due to diabetes complications. Eddie was in 1st grade and was a troubled little boy who needed a structured home with rules and discipline. His school principal reached out to me and told me that he was in danger of going into the system if we didn't take him. She even brought him to Louisiana and we met her there to pick him up.

Our living conditions in my husband's hometown were something I couldn't do anymore. There were several incidents at the school with my sons that made me feel like I was going to end up hurting somebody's child for bullying my sons. I also had threatened a principal because she didn't see anything wrong with a little girl spitting in my son's face (I may be saved but God isn't done with me yet). After that, I told my husband that we had to go to Tallahassee to find a place to live, that Saturday we went to Tallahassee and did not leave until we found a house to rent. I was so excited that we were getting out of Gretna.

2004-2006

We joined the Christian Heritage Church in 2004 and I started learning who I am in God on another level. I had gone to a prayer conference that the Healing and Prayer Ministry was giving. One of the prayer ministers prayed for me and afterward, she asked me if I had thought about joining the prayer team. I told her yes and she set up an appointment for my interview to join the team. Later that week a couple of the prayer team leaders interviewed me and that evening after they had prayed I received a call inviting me to become a part of the prayer team. One of the pastors was over the team for a time and then Pastor Mike took over. I learned so much from the leadership of both of these wonderful men of God. I didn't even know what my calling was at that time but the training I received was preparing me for being a Chaplain. I should have known because I absolutely loved being on the Healing and Prayer Ministry. Not long after joining the prayer ministry I began Seminary. This was one of the best things I could have ever done. I grew in biblical knowledge. Around this time my mother in law started letting her dislike for me show, by calling me and saying not so nice things to me usually when she had been drinking. I had told my husband that whatever happens between us he shouldn't call his mother and tell her because he could do no wrong in her eyes. I knew he wasn't telling her the things he was doing wrong in our marriage. One of the times she called Alvin was sitting right next to me and I gave him the phone so he could hear it firsthand. When he got a good earful of it he told her that if she couldn't respect his wife then she didn't need to call us ever again and he hung up the phone on her. I let him calm down then I told him that he needed to call her back because he only had one momma and I didn't want to be the cause of them not talking. I began to pray to ask God to change my relationship with my mother in law and I asked Him what I could do to help it change for the better. The Lord told me to go buy some of the blank greeting cards and to write prayers for my mother in love and her husband in them. He instructed me to start sending her a card once a week, so that's what I did and it changed our relationship. She told me that she still has those cards and she still reads them sometimes. She also calls me her daughter now and we have a better relationship.

Let's Pray:

Dear Heavenly Father, I ask You Lord to give this Princess peace when it comes to the relationship between her and her mother in love. Direct her on how to love her the way You love her. Touch the brokenness in the relationship and make it whole in You. Heal the hurt and help them both to be forgiving and full of grace. Give this Princess creative ideas on how to break down any walls that have been built between her and her mother in love. Give them mutual respect for the place they each hold in the heart of her husband. Help him to bring peace to the relationship as well and not feel like he is caught in the middle of his wife the Princess and his mother. I thank You for a new relationship between this Princess and her mother in love in Jesus' name, Amen.

Write a prayer for your mother in law even if you're not married yet start praying for your future mother in law and your relationship with her.

_____

_____

_____

_____

_____

_____

_____

_____

_____

_____

_____

_____

_____

_____

_____

_____

In 2005, I was arrested for something I didn't do. While working at the mental hospital an employee assaulted a resident and because I was the acting supervisor my name was brought into the situation, lies were told and I along with the staff member were accused of assault. I resigned my position after about a week of continuing to try to work in an environment that was very uncomfortable because of the accusations. A few weeks later I got a full-time job at my church in the school and one evening several months later I was on the way to the Christmas party at the church and I got pulled over by the police for speeding but when he came to my car window he said to me that there was a warrant out for my arrest. Needless to say, I was shocked because I hadn't gotten a letter or phone call stating anything about a warrant. The officer let me call my husband who was already at the church he came to where I was pulled over and got my belongings from me and talked to the officer. My husband was very upset but I was calm I said to the officer well praise the Lord let's go. The officer handcuffed me and put me in the backseat of his car as we were driving the officer was smoking a cigarette and I asked him to put it out he did and we talked he told me "this has to be a mistake I have never arrested anyone like you before." When we arrived at the Sheriff Department I was strip-searched (the whole spread your butt cheeks and cough) by a female cop who seemed to love her job just a little too much in my opinion. I was placed into a holding cell where there were already 3 other young women. When I walked in I said well bless the Lord my name is Tynika what are your names, they looked at me like I was crazy. But I knew that there was a bigger reason for why I was there. I had never been in trouble before let alone arrested for anything so there had to be a purpose to this. The ladies told me their names we talked and I was able to share with them the love of the Lord. They all asked me to pray for them so I did and I invited them to come to church when they were released. After sitting in the holding cell for several hours I was given a change of clothes and taken to a cell where there was a woman asleep on the bottom bunk. I got as comfortable as I could in that cold cell with a steel slate and a flat mat and wool blanket to try to get some rest. In the morning my cellmate woke up and we talked she explained to me the routine of the jail and we talked about God and read the Bible together. She asked me if I could call her mother when I got out and give her a message for her which I did. My husband came to visit me that morning to let me know that he was getting the money together to get me out, while he was there he told me how sexy I looked in my blue jailhouse uniform trying to make me laugh (it didn't work). I spent 17 hours in jail and of course, it felt like much longer. When Alvin and I got home I remember the boys asking me if I had been out ministering all night and I told them yes. That next day was Sunday and at the end of service two of the three ladies that I was in the holding cell with came up to me after church service to make sure I knew they had come, one of the ladies continued to attend the church. I ended up going through a nine-month ordeal with this case against me. I had to go to court every month. My church had called a very expensive lawyer to represent me. God did so many awesome things during that time that it would take too long to explain them all. During all of that, I was crying out to God asking him why me why did I have to go through this when I wasn't guilty of the things they were saying I did and God said to me so clearly "why not you?" He let me know that this was a process for me to learn to trust Him completely. Well at the end of it all I had to go to a jury trial I picked my jury and we broke for lunch. When my husband and I got back to the courthouse we were sitting in the car waiting for the time to go back into the courtroom and my lawyer called me on my cell phone and told me that he had some good news for me. He came outside and met us on the sidewalk with a piece of paper in his hand. It was from the district attorney stating that they had dropped all charges against me! All I could do was praise God! Through all of it, the Lord kept telling me that I wasn't going to jail but my circumstances looked different. On September 14th, 2006 the Lord gave me

Isaiah 42:5-10 and told me that was my call. I had to learn to trust God completely. I learned that when you take that vow to serve God saying "yes Lord I'll go where you want me to go, I'll say what you want me to say, I'll do what you want me to do", you better be ready to be put into some situations that are very uncomfortable, hard, dark times that you may not be able to see the light at the end of the tunnel. My church at the beginning of this whole thing had told me that they were going to help me with the lawyer but in the end, they didn't help pay for anything. God wouldn't let them because He wanted me to trust Him only and that's what I did. We didn't have to pay the lawyer anything they did it for free after much prayer that went forth. After all of that, I had a meeting with the district attorney who had been trying to put me in prison and he told me that if I ever needed him to give me a recommendation that he would vouch for my good character. My pastor had me to tell him my testimony then at the New Year's Eve service I shared my testimony with the entire church. My husband's Aunt Glenda was there and asked if I could come to share my testimony at her church as well. God truly showed me that He is El Olam (My Everlasting God).

Let's Pray:

Gracious and Heavenly Father I come to You asking You to be with every Princess that has ever or will ever be put in a situation where they are falsely accused of a crime. Give them the strength, wisdom, peace of mind, intercessors and support they need to get through the trials. Help her to know that You will never leave her nor forsake her in Jesus' name. Lord while she goes through the process; show her what is on the inside of her that needs to come out. Teach her how to pray, when to pray, and what scriptures to stand on. Lord, help Your Princess to be a light in the dark situation and the atmosphere changer in what looks like a prison cell. Father, help her to not believe what it looks like but to trust that You will work it out for her good and Your glory in Jesus' name. Lord if anyone disappoints her through this process; help her to realize that You want her to put her trust in You and only You. Father, I thank You for her testimony of how You brought her through in Jesus' name, Amen.

Have you been put in a situation
where you were accused of something
you didn't do? Did you have a good
support system? Write a prayer asking
God for strength, peace and a good
support group when you go through a
storm.

_____

_____

_____

_____

_____

_____

_____

_____

_____

_____

_____

_____

2007

In 2007 I was at church praying at the altar when a young woman came to the altar asking our pastor's wife to pray for her. I had never seen her before and didn't know her story but I felt a tugging in my heart to pray for her so I prayed and later was told that she was a single mother of two young daughters and she was battling breast cancer. Within the next day or two I had received our prayer list email and her name was on the hospital visitation list. I proceeded to pray for her and the Lord spoke to me and told me to go to the hospital and pray with her. I proceeded to tell God that my praying for her right there at home was good enough because I didn't like going to the hospital. Well God and I went back and forth a couple of times until I said yes Lord and I went to the hospital. I found her hospital room fairly easily and she was actually right outside her room just getting back from having chemotherapy. I introduced myself and told her why I was there. She and I talked for a while then I prayed for her and gave her my telephone number so she could call me if she needed anything. This was the start of an awesome move of God. She had lost both her jobs due to the illness. She and the girls had to move in with her mother and stepfather which she told me was a very stressful situation. She had been storing all of her belongings in her mother's garage and they had been ruined due to rain. Her father had come to help her get an apartment after she had a double mastectomy but they had nothing to put in the apartment. Well the Lord had me to share this information with a friend and we felt led to contact the Caring Connections of the Tallahassee Democrat. A reporter called me and set up an appointment with the young lady to take pictures of her and to tell her story. The story was to be in the newspaper in the middle of November. When that day came the article wasn't in the paper so I called the reporter to find out what happened and she told me that her editor was so moved by the story that she was going to run it on Thanksgiving Day!! Thanksgiving came and on the front page of the Tallahassee Democrat was a picture of her and the words "God Will Provide."

The article told her story and asked people for donations of furniture, clothing, household items and whatever else they could give to this single mother of two fighting breast cancer and my name and information was there as the point of contact. This was all before "Go fund me" accounts. My family and I had gone to my husband's grandmother's house for dinner and by the time we got home the front door was flooded with blessings and on my door was a note from the mayor of Tallahassee with all his telephone numbers asking me to call him. I did call his home and he asked me to bring the young lady to meet him. The gifts kept coming so much so that I had to set up an account for her at the bank and my garage was over flowing with extra furniture. The Lord put on our hearts to bless others with the overflow. So out of the overflow a ministry called 3rd Day Missions Inc. was born. After the story came out in the newspaper I was invited several times to be on a local television show called Live @ 45 hosted by Pastor Sheppard I was also invited to pray and minister at different churches over the years.

Let's pray:

Father in the name of Jesus I come to You asking You to touch this Princess. Help her to have creative ideas on how to help the people You put in her path. Show her how to minister, pray, and bless everyone You send her way. I also ask You that anyone she knows whether it's her or a loved one that is battling cancer that You are sending Your holy fire to devour every cancerous cell in their body right now in Jesus' name. I thank You Lord that they will live and not die to declare the great works of the Lord. Thank You Lord that You are a provider and healer and You are able to do everything that is needed to be done. We thank You in Jesus' name, Amen.

Has God called you to start a ministry? What is the goal of the ministry? Who are you going to help? Write a prayer asking God for direction and then write what you hear so you can get started.

_____

_____

_____

_____

_____

_____

_____

_____

_____

_____

_____

_____

_____

2008-2010

Through the years my husband continually talked about he wanted us to move to Atlanta that he felt God was leading us there. I would tell him you are acting like Moses trying to lead us to the "Promise Land." I continually told him no because I didn't want to raise my 5 black sons in Atlanta or even around it because it was too dangerous. In 2008 Alvin ended up losing both of his jobs in Florida, our house went into foreclosure and the church began to split all within less than a year. Alvin started coming here to the Atlanta area to look for a job. My Aunt Terry (Eddie's grandmother) was asking me if Eddie could come spend Christmas with her that year. I was very hesitant but she and he wore me down and I allowed him to go to Kansas for Christmas. Now let me give a quick background about my Aunt Terry: as much as I loved her she was a hot mess. She was not a very honest person and she had a drug problem for most of my life. Now don't get me wrong I loved her very much but I didn't trust her as far as I could throw her. Alvin, I and our other boys went to Miami to spend Christmas with my husband's father and step mother. While we were there I had a dream that someone's house was being broken into while they were away. When Eddie got back from Kansas we could tell something had changed in him. When we first got Eddie he couldn't read and could barely write his name. We worked with him and showed him a structured life treating him like one of our own. Everything our sons got he got too. He had been around people that weren't very good influences on him. He thought the "thug life" was a great lifestyle. I remember one incident we had went to Walmart and as we were leaving the store the door alarms started going off. We couldn't figure out what was making it go off so the lady at the door let us leave. When we got home I searched and searched him but couldn't find anything. Later that evening one of the boys seen a pair of earrings that he had stolen, when we asked him why he had stolen the earrings he said that he wanted to look good. When he had first come to our home he had an earring in his ear and I made him take it out because that wasn't something we allowed in our home. After Eddie came back from Kansas he became defiant and I knew my aunt had something to do with it. One day he went to school and after he came home there was a knock on our door, it was a social worker from DFC's. He told me that he had gotten a call from the school saying that Eddie had told the teacher that he was afraid to come home because my husband threaten to choke and beat him. I couldn't believe it at first but then it all made sense. My aunt had told him that she wanted him back and all the fun things they would do when he came back to live with her. So she had him tell his teacher a lie so he could come live with her. I let the social worker do everything he needed to do and I told him Eddie's history and how we ended up having custody of him then I told the social worker to take him. He looked at me like I was crazy and I said again take him with you because if he wants to go back to his grandma that bad that he would lie and put my family in jeopardy then either you take him or I will put him on a plane back to Kansas as soon as school is over (which was a couple of weeks away). The social worker told me not to do that because our home was the best place for him. I agreed with him but I wasn't going to have a defiant child in my home that would lie and do whatever they thought they needed to do to get out of my home. After the social worker left I sat Eddie down and asked him why he lied like that. Did he want to go live with his grandma that bad that he would lie on us like that and he said yes. He said he wanted to go back to his grandma's house in Kansas. I asked Eddie a couple of times before we bought him a plane ticket if he was sure because if he left our home we were not going to let him come back to live with us again. Each time we asked him he said yes he wanted to go. I talked to other family members and everyone said it was a bad idea but they understood that I wasn't going to allow Eddie to put my other children in a bad situation. I talked to my aunt and let her know that Eddie was coming back to live with her that she got her way. I told her how we had him in counseling and that she needed to continue his therapy because he had been diagnosed with a couple of things. She told me that he didn't need therapy and that I had made her grandson "soft". The very next day after school was out for the summer we drove Eddie to Atlanta to the airport and sent him to Kansas to live. From the time we got Eddie to the time he left our home he had gone from not being able to read to winning awards at school for reading. I hated seeing him leave because I knew the environment he was going to wasn't going to be healthy. He ended up getting in trouble not long after he moved back to Kansas. We keep him in our prayers.

Let's Pray:

Father in the name of Jesus I lift up all troubled children and family members of the Princess reading this book. I ask You, Lord, to bring structure and stability to their lives in the name of Jesus. Place the right people in the lives of the children to show them the love of Christ and give the children self-control and self-worth. Show the children how to love themselves and respect others. Lord, place them in the classroom of the teacher You have trained and designed just for them in Jesus' precious mighty name, Amen.

Do you know any children that are having issues because of a loss of a parent? Write a prayer for them and the person raising them.

_____

_____

_____

_____

_____

_____

_____

_____

_____

_____

_____

_____

_____

I was praying the morning after I graduated from seminary in December of 2009 asking God what I was supposed to do because He knew I did not want to be a pastor. I heard so clearly "you are to be a Chaplain" well my only encounter with a Chaplain was the military Chaplain that married my sister-cousin Linda and her husband. I told the Lord I am not going into the military. I started doing research on how to become a Chaplain to figure out what I needed to do and what other training I needed. Eventually Alvin moved to Atlanta and lived with his cousin and his family. He got a job and we moved here to Atlanta on January 1st 2010. I had planned on finding a church, just sitting on the pew and not really getting involved because I had been so heavily involved in church for the past seven years and went through so much hurt and pain that I just wanted to take a break. We were here in this area for about a month and I got invited to Global Impact Christian Ministries by my supervisor on my first day of work, so I went on that Wednesday to bible study and really enjoyed to word and how Pastor Spence broke it down so that my children could understand it. My supervisor introduced me to Pastor Spence we talked and I told him about myself and my family. That Sunday my family came to church and my husband met the pastor and invited him and his family over for dinner and we prayed together. From there I was asked by pastor to start an intercessory prayer ministry needless to say that blew my plans out the window of being a pew warmer. Being in this leadership position taught me a lot. There were a couple of women on the team that were difficult and that taught me how to handle difficult people in ministry.

2011-2013

In February of 2011 I was in my first unit of CPE (Clinical Pastoral Education the training for Chaplains) and I had written my story. This brought up a lot of different emotions and memories for me. I wanted to know who I was biologically and as a person. Knowing that there was a question about if Tony really was my biological dad had me feeling all kinds of emotions. I started asking questions to anyone and everyone I could think of that might know something. I contacted a childhood friend that I thought his father maybe my dad and he told me "No my dad was your mom's pimp I thought you knew that." I was shocked but not shock because then a lot of memories I must have suppressed came flooding back to me. I remembered the white house with the red porch light my mother lived in that "Nigga Mary" (the Madame of the house) ran for her son who was the pimp, my mom's pimp! I had suppressed the fact that my mother was a prostitute. My mind for many years had me remembering that she was his girlfriend not his "ho". My Aunt Terri had told me there was another possible person and I reached out to his sister who in turn asked him and he said he had never had sex with my mother. This had me feeling confused and empty until God put in my spirit the scripture Ephesians 1:5. Even though I don't know for sure yet if Tony is my biological dad I have some peace in knowing he loved me as his own no matter the outcome.

Let's Pray:

Father in the name of Jesus I come to You asking You Lord to help Your Princesses who have experienced an identity crisis because of her parent's carelessness. Help her to know that You chose her before You created this world to be blameless and holy in Your sight. Lord, help her to know that You predestined her for adoption through Jesus Christ and that it is Your will and pleasure. Show her that You know her name and the number of hairs on her head because You created her in love regardless of the sins of her parents. Thank You, Father, for her identity being in You in Jesus' name, Amen.

Do you know your father? Have you been lied to about your parents? If it's not you do you know someone who has questions about their parents? Write a prayer asking God to show them who they are in Him and for them to get peace where they don't get the answers.

_____

_____

_____

_____

_____

_____

_____

_____

_____

_____

_____

March 10th of 2011 I was well into the first month of my first unit of CPE. I was figuring out who I was and what my story was at that time. What makes Tynika do, feel, and be who she is, was the main question on my mind. I wanted to bring closure to some painful areas of my life through confronting some people and forgiving the pain they caused. One of those main people was the uncle that raped and molested me. I reached out to him on Facebook and wrote him a message @ 6:45pm saying: *I wanted to let you know that I am writing a book about my life. I want to know if you are ready to talk about the secrets our family has kept for years. It's up to you whether or not you want to talk about it. Regardless my book will be written and my story told. So let me know if you are ready to talk. Also this book is my story, my life. I am not writing it to make anyone feel guilty or bad because the Lord has healed me but I need to get to the root of the problem so I can pray that God breaks the chains of bondage off of our family! I know that someone molested and raped you and that a lot of crazy crap happened in grandma's house this crap has been going on for generations. It's a curse in our family that has to be stopped! I know that my mother was a prostitute but what happened to her to make her make that decision in life? There are a lot of secrets and demons that are going to be exposed. Well I hope to hear from you soon, if not that's fine too cause I'm still praying for you and have already forgiven you. Love you with the love of Christ....Tynika*

I was thinking I had sent him a nice message letting him know what my plans were in writing a book but also letting him know that I had forgiven him. I waited for his reply thinking it was going to be one telling me that he was sorry for what he had done to me when I was a child. Instead of my uncle reply he made up some Facebook profile for 'Kindle Law Kindle" and replied this message to me: *Hello Mrs. Baker-Isaac, You don't know me, but some important information has been brought to my attention by a client of mine. It seems you are making some false claims of rape and other sexual claims that are not true. It has also been brought to my attention that you took part in some childhood explicit expressions of your own by calling him down to the basement to partake with you on several different occasions. You claim your deceased mother was a hooker. Why would you not allow her to rest in peace? It is clear you need to seek immediate mental help for your condition. The choice to write a book is your own, but PLEASE be careful, don't allow someone the opportunity to have you in court for defamation of one's present reputation. Slanderous statements you can't prove are illegal in America. It was said that you're a smart woman, and you should find a way to move past your childhood expressions that you made happen yourself several times by constantly calling my client down to the basement on your own. It was not just him and you know it. I'm supposed to ask if you plan to mention that in your book. My suggestion to you is that you don't use any names or information about anyone you can't prove in a court of law to keep yourself out of a court of law Mrs. Baker-Isaac.*

I was both livid and amused when I read this message it made me laugh and cuss at the same time. I couldn't believe how stupid he thought I was to think a lawyer would contact me through Facebook but also that he said I as a child asked to be raped and molested over and over again by him. He didn't realize that he basically confessed to raping me. I wanted to immediately reply to him but my husband talked me down and told me to take some time to think about how I wanted to respond to him. I took about 12 hours to ponder about what I was going to say back to him. This is what I said: *Mr. Kindle Law Kindle aka (my uncle's full name) as you stated in your message to me I am a VERY SMART woman and I am smart enough to know that any reputable legal lawyer would not reply to me on behalf of their client by email or Facebook IT WOULD BE BY CERTIFIED LETTER! I laughed out loud when I read it that you thought that you could intimidate me with this ignorant not well thought out reply. For you to say to me that I as a child 10 years younger than you voluntarily partook in your sick sexual acts of raping me shows me and anyone else that You (uncle's name) is* the one that CLEARLY NEEDS TO SEEK IMMEDIATE MENTAL HELP! I welcome your frivolous lawsuit just like the lawsuits you filed against Target and Publisher's Clearing House this too would be thrown out of court but not after I have called to speak on my behalf every last person you have victimized. Oh yes I have names and have been in contact with these people so if you want to play let's get it on! You need to wake up and take a real long good look in the mirror! (UNCLE'S FULL NAME) YOU ARE A CONVICTED RAPIST and it seems to me that those almost 8 years you spent behind bars did not help you realize you have a problem and that to me is very scary because you are very well probably still preying on victims! I do thank you for the reply *because that gives me a great quote word for word that I am going to put in my book with your name next to it Kindle Law Kindle aka (my uncle's name). Again I have forgiven you and the fact that you choose to live in denial helps me to know what to pray for when it comes to you. I pray that God will allow everything that needs to happen to get you where God wants you to be in Him will happen in your life. I still love you with the love of Christ, Tynika.*

My uncle never replied back to me but we will see if he sues me for writing about what he did to me in this book. I didn't mention his name so if he sues it's just another admission of guilt.

Let's Pray:

Father in the mighty name of Jesus I lift up every Princess that has been victimized and chooses to stand up to her abuser. Give her the strength to speak her words and to be strong and courageous. Lord, whether Your Princess chooses to confront or not to confront her abuser help her to have the peace she needs to move forward in freedom knowing that she did not ask for the abuse or do anything to warrant it. Father, deal with the abuser don't allow them to rest until they repent and get in right standing with You even if they never admit their guilt to the victim or a court in Jesus' name, Amen.

Do you know someone that is a victim of crime and needs healing? Do you know someone who has victimized someone but has no remorse? Write a prayer for the victim and the offender.

_____

_____

_____

_____

_____

_____

_____

_____

_____

_____

_____

_____

_____

Living here in Atlanta I had "friends" but I didn't have the prayer partner connection with any of them like I did with the three women in Hinesville. In March of 2011 the Lord laid on my heart to find Sheila, Vernell, and Carmen my three prayer partners that I worked with over 10 years ago at Walmart in Hinesville. I had lost contact with them and hadn't talked to them in years. I found each one of them within days of each other. I called each one of them and got caught up with what had been going on with them through the years. I prayed and sought the Lord on why He wanted me to find them and He told me so that we could pray together again. I asked him how we were supposed to do that when we're all in different cities and one in a different state and I heard "freeconferencecall.com, start a prayer call with your new and old prayer partners and call your selves "The Powerful Praying Princesses". I was blown away and excited to get started. So that's what I did. I informed all of the ladies I prayed with to get on the call and we prayed and are still praying together at 5:30am Monday-Friday and at 9:30 pm every night Monday-Sunday. Of course some of the ladies have fallen off the call, some have started their own prayer calls and we've gotten new people that join and are times I maybe the only person on the call but the call has been going ever since 2011. Anyone can join us and we even get men that get on the call and pray with us. You can find the prayer call information in the back of the book, please join us.

Let's pray:

Lord, I thank You that You can use anyone to do Your will here on earth. I ask You, Lord, to touch Your Princess and give her the gift and spirit of intercession. I ask You to urge her to join her faith with her sisters The Powerful Praying Princesses and get on the call with us to pray and seek Your will for our lives, our families, and this world. Thank You, Lord, that You are giving her the sisterhood of The Powerful Praying Princesses to encourage her, and help her grow in her faith in You in Jesus' name, Amen.

Do you have any friends or enemies that you want to bless by giving them the Powerful Praying Princesses call information and inviting them to get on the call? Write a list of friends/enemies and send them the number also write a prayer for their hearts to receive the invitation to join the call in love. 515-603-4924 access code 257640# @5:30am/9:30pm EDT

_____

_____

_____

_____

_____

_____

_____

_____

_____

I was in my 2nd unit of CPE when I received a phone call on the night of December 7th. It was my cousin Sharon (mom's cousin that lived across the street from my dad) calling to tell me that no one had heard from my dad for a few days and my Aunt Hollye (dad's sister) had called the police to do a welfare check on him at his house and the police had found him dead on the floor right by the front door in his house. I couldn't believe it, now my dad was dead too. I felt immediately like an orphan. It was crazy I really never had a strong, great relationship with either of my parents but I felt like I had lost the father of the year. I felt every emotion from sadness to anger. I also began analyzing myself because I had been studying and researching the stages of grief and the effects of it on people (remember I was in training for Chaplaincy). So many of my family members had died before this but I wasn't in this field so I had never really paid attention to peoples responses like I did then and now. When I went home (back to Emporia) for the funeral I stayed with my cousin Sharon and her husband Arthur. My Aunt Hollye and I had the task of cleaning out my dad's house which was a shack and most everything went in the trash. I had been in my dad's house several times before but cleaning it made me feel so sad for him. The fact that he literally had nothing of value and that he died alone and had probably been dead for several days before he was discovered hurt my heart. After I got home to

Atlanta from my dad's funeral I was talking to his mom on the phone I said to her "Grandma, dad told me that you didn't think I was his biological child" and she said to me "Yes that's true Tynika and I still don't think you are." I replied trying to get her to think otherwise "But Grandma my mom got pregnant (the summer of 8th grade) when she was only 14 years old. I'm sure she remembered who she had sex with." Grandma said "hmm well Tyni me and your grandpa said it wasn't your fault so we treated you like ours and picked you up for visits." I ended the conversation with "Yes, you're my grandma and always will be."

My Aunt Hollye was always around when I was growing up. She would pick me up from grandma's house and ride me on her bike across town to her mom's house so I could visit with that side of my family. She hung out at my house all the time partying with my mom's family and everyone loved her. She never had any biological children but she treated all children like her own. I was in my 20's when I told her about me being molested and raped and the words that came out of her mouth shocked the crap out of me! She said "I tried to protect you from that. That's why I came and got you all the time to keep you away from there. I'm sorry I couldn't protect you Tyni." This made me feel like a lot more people knew about what was happening to me while growing up and nobody did anything to stop it or protect me. You know how families have those "family secrets" and that attitude that "what happens in this house stays in this house." This attitude is why so many children continually get raped and molested and no one finds out about it until that child is acting out and a lot of times not even then because people see that child as the problem and not that there is a reason why she is being promiscuous.

Let's pray:

Father in the name of Jesus I ask You to touch the heart of every Princess that has lost her dad. Lord, You are the only One that can fill the hole in her heart from this loss. Help her to know that she is not an orphan and that You have adopted her into Your family. Let her feel Your loving presence and send Your Holy Spirit to comfort her. Father if there is any question of her paternity ease her mind in knowing that she has Your DNA and that You are the Father! I thank You Lord that negative words don't change Your love for her and her identity in You in Jesus' name, Amen.

Have you lost your father whether through death or abandonment or do you know someone who has lost a father? Write a prayer asking our Heavenly Father to intervene in their life.

_____

_____

_____

_____

_____

_____

_____

_____

_____

_____

_____

_____

May of 2013 both Christian and Davian graduated high school. I was so excited yet sad that two of my sons were "grown." Davian went on to college for a year but that turned out not to be his "cup of tea" which was a very hard thing for me to handle because I have always stressed to my sons how important it is to have a college degree. I have to trust God with my son's decisions in life and trust that my husband and I have raised them right and they will be successful productive citizens. Davian is walking out his journey in life. I try not to worry about him because he is my prodigal child. He says that he doesn't know if there is a God and of course as a mother that is a strong believer in Christ to hear that come out of my son's mouth was a very hard thing. But I have to continue to pray for him and trust God's word which says in Proverbs 22:6 (NKJV) "Train up a child in the way he should go, and when he is old he will not depart from it." Christian is special needs and mentally is very much delayed. Christian loves people and wants to talk to everyone so we keep a close eye on him. He has a worker that takes him out into the community to work with him and help him fill out applications. He had a job for about a month at McDonald's but it didn't work out for him there.

Let's Pray:

Father, in the name of Jesus I lift up every prodigal child of every Princess and I ask You Lord to touch their lives. Help them to see that You are God and that You are real. Show them Your love, forgiveness, and patience. Lord, I pray that You save their souls, that You not let them die and go to hell but that You save them so that they will have everlasting life with You. Father, I thank You that You are giving every mom peace that passes all understanding in knowing You have their children in Your hands because You Lord are concerned about everything that concerns us as mothers of the children You blessed us with. We thank You, Lord, that You love them more than we do and that's a lot. Father thank You and we trust You Lord in Jesus' name, Amen.

Do you have a child or know someone who has a child that doesn't believe in God and Jesus Christ? Write a prayer for the condition of heart and for God to send the right person into their life to minister to them.

_____

_____

_____

_____

_____

_____

_____

_____

_____

_____

_____

_____

_____

August of 2013 I completed a Chaplaincy Residency at Emory University Hospital and began looking for a full time Chaplain position. I had a friend who was the Chaplain for a small hospice and he asked me if I would volunteer for a couple of hours a week. I was looking to make some money but I also loved being a Chaplain and told him I would. My friend ended up resigning from the position and I was hired on as the Chaplain. Later that year in November Aunt Hollye died of breast cancer. I went home for her funeral and was staying with my cousin Eva when she called me from work telling me I needed to go check on Sharon and to take her to the hospital because she was sick and refusing to go. When I got to Sharon's which was a block away I told Sharon she was going to the hospital even if I had to pick her up and carry her to the car myself she said "ok Tyni" but then she said "can we wait until the Young and the Restless goes off." I said okay and we watched it together then I took her to the hospital. She was diagnosed with cirrhosis of the liver and a couple of days after I got back to Atlanta I received a phone call from my cousin Eva telling me that Sharon had been diagnosed with liver cancer and was put on hospice. Sharon died Dec.31, 2013.

2014-2015

At the end of 2014, I decided to go back to college and went back in February of 2015 to get a degree in Psychology. I think my grandmother always telling me I wasn't anything made me an overachiever later in life which is something I am still trying to get delivered from. I have put too much stress on myself to be better or do more.

The end of May or June Sheila and I were praying and the Lord spoke that "something major was going to happen in a few weeks that was going to change my life." Sheila began praising God but I felt complete devastation. I couldn't shake the feeling that something bad was going to happen in my life. I tried to continue to go about my daily activities but in the back of my mind, I kept wondering what was going to happen and when was it going to happen. Alvin started drinking more than he had been and coming home later from work than normal. One night he hadn't come home and I kept calling his cell phone and it was going to voice mail then I would call his work number and no one answered. I was worried and my sons were asking me where dad was and all I could tell them was that he was at work not knowing where he was. When he finally came home I wanted to punch him in the face when I realized he was drunk but I didn't say a word to him. I prayed and asked God what to do and I was instructed to write him a letter telling him that if he didn't stop I was leaving and taking the boys with me. The next day I gave him the letter and he apologized to me and the boys and said he was going to stop drinking. A day or two later it happened! Please understand this was a very traumatic life-changing experience for me and my husband. A lot of the conversations and memories of this time are kind of like a blur of time mixed all together. All of these events happened within a week and it's hard for me to remember everything because I was in shock.

Sheila and I were praying one morning before I went to work and the Lord said that "Alvin was having inappropriate conversations with a woman at work." I was upset; Sheila tried to calm me down. I told her I would call her back and I called Alvin. The first thing I said to him was "WHO IS SHE!?" He acted like he didn't know what I was talking about and said who is who I went on to tell him that I was praying and what the Lord revealed. He said they were flirting but nothing else. I got off the phone with him and called Sheila back to pray again while praying the Lord gave me more information telling me that it was more than just flirting but that Alvin had been having an affair with a woman at work. I called him back and told him what God revealed and of course, he denied it but I knew it was true. One of my first thoughts was what were our sons going to think. Throughout our marriage, I had been having dreams that he was having sex with other women and of course, God wouldn't lie. There had been things he had said and done that made me wonder "why did he say that" or "where did he get that position from we never done that before." I am at work by now driving to see my patients

I can remember at times I couldn't stop crying then other times it seemed like I had no more tears to cry. It was very hard to focus on my patients and families while dealing with my own crisis. (At this time I was a Chaplain for a hospice and I traveled to different patient's homes for visits.) I was beyond angry I was livid. I kept thinking about how is this going to change who my sons are supposed to be if they find out. I couldn't let my sons find out, I had to stay calm and get the boys out of the house. I needed someone to talk to me that would not take sides but would be honest with me and gentle because I was broken and I also knew he was someone that would talk to my husband and help us figure this mess out. I knew he would give me godly counsel and understanding. So I called my mentor and friend Pastor Michael Smith to tell him what was going on. He couldn't believe it but very calmly he asked me "Well what are you going to do?" I told him I didn't know then I think I told him I was going to leave Alvin. He talked to me and helped me to stop and think before acting on my emotions. He asked me what role I played in all of it. He didn't accuse me of anything or make me feel like it was my fault but he wanted me to stop and think. I know I have always been a strong independent person but that's no reason to cheat. I asked Pastor Mike to call Alvin and talked to him. I found out later the just of that conversation was him telling Alvin that he needed to be honest with me, tell me everything and allow me to decide whether or not I was going to stay or leave. I called Sheila again and I don't even remember the conversation, but I know she prayed for me because I couldn't pray for myself. After Pastor Mike and Alvin's conversation Alvin called me and told me that we needed to talk when he got home.

Let's Pray:

Father in the name of Jesus I ask You to place a Holy Spirit-filled mentor and confidant in the life of Your Princess. Lord, give Your Princess the trust she needs in the person so she can be honest and transparent with them. I thank You, Father, that You did not create Your children to be alone but to have each other to help carry the load. Lord, give this Princess's husband the same respect for the mentor to be able, to be honest with them too. Also, put a person in her husband's life that will hold him accountable and mentor him as well. Thank You, Father, for Your in Jesus' name, Amen.

Do you have a mentor/confidant that you check in with on a regular basis, who tells you the truth in love even if it hurts? If you don't write a prayer asking God to send that person into your life but if you do write a prayer covering that person and your relationship.

_____

_____

_____

_____

_____

_____

_____

_____

_____

_____

_____

When I got home from work that day I asked the boys if they wanted to go to Florida for a couple of weeks for a vacation and of course they said yes. Thank God it was summer time so I called Alvin's Aunt Glenda and ask her if the boys could come to Florida for a couple of weeks for vacation and she told me she didn't think so because she had things to do and I begged her and she said to me "you're not going to kill my nephew are you?" I was shocked and I couldn't believe she said that because it had crossed my mind and a lot of other things too. I told the boys to pack a bag and that they were going to go to Florida for a couple of weeks for a vacation. I needed them to leave because I didn't know what I was going to say or do to Alvin when he got home.

I also didn't want them to find out what their father had done to their mother because I didn't want it to change who they were supposed to be and how they looked at the father whom they adored and respected. I went to the bank and took all the money out of the account and put it into my own account. I wanted to have the money to do what I needed to do. I gave the boys some money and sent them to Florida. After the boys left I was able to sit down and fall apart. It felt like someone had died. Like my husband or at least the man I thought my husband was died that day. I couldn't believe God allowed my husband of 18 years who I had been faithful to, cheat on me! We had been through this before and after that first time he told me, he promised me that he wouldn't hurt me like that again! I couldn't believe the husband I thought loved me so much cheated on me again. I felt so stupid and used. I was angry! I was angry at God and Alvin. I felt like the wind had been knocked out of me and I couldn't catch my breath. I couldn't even pray; I didn't even know how to pray anymore. I was so confused. You know that confusion you feel when you're told that someone you love died unexpectedly. I didn't know this person I spent 18 years of my life with and gave him my heart! Now I'm shattered into pieces! I realize now that I began grieving a marriage I thought I had and lost.

While I was waiting on Alvin to get home Sheila called me to check on me and told me that she had been praying for me and that I was to stay with Alvin because the Lord was going to use us and our story to help other married couples, that this is our ministry. I told her no it's not fair. Why do I have to stay? Why do I have to humble myself and forgive Alvin when he got to have his cake and eat it too. I told her I wasn't trying to hear it and I was leaving. She said, "Ty I'm just giving you what God gave me." This made me even angrier that God said I had to not only forgive Alvin but stay with him too! God knows I trust Sheila and if she tells me God said something I know He said it. Sheila prays more than anyone I know and she has said countless things that have come to pass. But I wasn't trying to hear anything anyone had to say about staying with Alvin, not even God. But I kept thinking about my sons and what it would do to them to uproot them and have to explain why. It wasn't fair that Alvin would be getting everything I felt he didn't deserve if I stay. He made his choices and done the wrong but I felt I was being put in a situation to right his wrongs and it wasn't fair!

When Alvin arrived home from work I was sitting at the dining room table I had just got done taking a hand saw and sawing a wooden double heart with our names in each heart into two pieces. He walked up to me and said "hit me" I told him to get out of my face and he said it again "just hit me.... do something." I couldn't, as much as I wanted to punch him in the throat the

Holy Spirit wouldn't let me. I just sat there and cried telling him how disappointed and hurt I was. (Right then I knew I was really saved and a new creature in Christ because the old Tynika would have bashed his head in as angry and hurt I was.)

That first night alone in the house with Alvin, I made him sleep downstairs on the couch and I locked our bedroom door. I cried myself to sleep and I don't think I got much sleep at all because my mind was racing with questions and thinking of the signs I seen but ignored: Why didn't I see this earlier? Why was I so stupid? What's wrong with me? My life for the past 18 years had been all a lie and big fat fraud! Why me God why did you allow this to happen to me? I kept thinking about Alvin having sex with another woman. I remembered the times he stopped answering his cell phone while he was at work and he started coming home from work later and later. This is why he didn't want me to buy a gun when I told him I was buying one for my protection because I traveled a lot alone for work. I had thought about calling my friend who owns a crematorium and telling her to fire it up because I have a body. My mind was all over the place. I wanted to know why. Why did God allow this to happen to me and how could my husband the man I adored do this to me? What was broken in him that would make him feel this was acceptable behavior? Of course, there was nothing he could say to me that would justify the pain I was feeling.

Both of us still had to go to work so that meant he was going to be around this woman for 8-10 hours every day and that truly messed with my mind. I said to him that I hated that he was still spending time with her and he was wearing the cologne I bought him. He asked me if I wanted him to quit work. I knew we needed that income but I thought at what cost.   Alvin told me after he had returned home from going to the gas station that God spoke to him and told him he couldn't continue to do his daughter like this and gave him a vision of a lake of fire and told him that if he continued down the road he was on he was going to end up dead The Lord also told him that he had to come completely clean with me and tell me the whole truth. As he told me everything my heart continued to break. I couldn't understand why I wasn't enough. I never withheld affection from him. I always told him I loved him. Yes, I have always been an independent woman but he told me that he admired that about me. I kept asking myself "Why wasn't I enough?" I allowed the enemy to truly play with my mind and had me focusing on every flaw I could find in myself. It truly was a battle in my mind and at times still is hard for me. Through the next week, Alvin and I talked more than we had talked in years. He shared with me how he was angry at God and jealous of me. He was jealous that God was using me in ministry more than him. He also shared that he was insecure; he didn't like certain physical things about himself. Even though I see flaws in myself I still couldn't understand that a man as fine as my husband was so insecure. Although he had insecurities I was angry even though I understood what he was saying there was no excuse for his infidelities. Throughout the next week or so we talked a lot at home and while we were at work; I'd be driving to visit a patient and call him and just go off on him yelling and screaming and crying. Once I even made him put the woman on the phone and I talked to her I can't remember exactly what all I said to her but I do remember Alvin asked me what I said because she was scared to stay at work and he begged me not to come to the job and cause a scene. That made me even angrier because I thought he was protecting her. He let me know real quick that he didn't want me to end up in jail. About two weeks later Alvin was called for jury duty. He spent a few days at the courthouse waiting to see if he was going to have to serve on the jury. He ended up not having to serve but during that time I let him know that I didn't want him to return to the job so he resigned. We knew that financially it was not going to be good for us but we also knew that if we were going to work on our marriage he couldn't stay at that job. Pastor Mike told him if we stayed together that Alvin couldn't minister to me through this pain because he caused it.

Let's Pray:

Father in the mighty name of Jesus I ask You to give this Princess strength and perseverance to get through the storms of life. Give her a Holy Spirit-filled prayer partner that will be honest and help her make sound decisions and not react to the pain of life but respond the way You direct her to. Give her self-control to not do anything that will send her to jail because You haven't called her to the prison ministry but help her to be focused on Your will for her life even through this storm. Thank You, Father in Jesus' name, Amen.

Is there an honest conversation you need to have with your husband or another person in your life? Write a prayer asking God to direct you in knowing how to address the issues and setting up the opportunity to have the conversation.

_____

_____

_____

_____

_____

_____

_____

_____

_____

_____

_____

The whole time we were going through this I was still going to work every day. I had to sit and listen to other people's problems and issues while my own house had seemed to have fallen apart. I felt like such a hypocrite, like a fraud because we were in church every Sunday and Wednesday and any other day the doors were open serving God and I had been running the Powerful Praying Princesses prayer call every day for years and here I am completely broken but still encouraging and praying for others. I kept moving forward in my pain not telling but a couple of people I trusted and knew that they would pray for me and not gossip about us. I remember one of the ladies in our church came up to me and said something like this "I admire you and your husband so much. Just watching you worship and praise God together is so beautiful. I want a relationship just like yours." I told her no honey you want the relationship God has for you. Don't ever want what others have because you don't know the hell they had to go through to get it. You never know what happens behind the closed doors of someone's home.

Alvin and I had to be completely honest with each other about everything that had happened in our marriage up to that point. We both had to come clean about our feelings and our life with each other. I let him know that I had reconnected with an ex-boyfriend and although our conversations were never more than catching up it was something I should not have hidden from my husband. We both had to decide whether we were going to stay together and work on our marriage or get a divorce. I had a hard time getting to the point of staying because I kept thinking what are people going to think of me? How can I stay with this man that has cheated on me numerous times and I have forgiven him before only for him to do it again. What if he does it again? What is a relationship without trust and can I ever trust him again? What about our sons, how would a divorce affect them? I'm not a woman that believes that parents should stay together for the kids because I've seen people with both parents in the home more messed up than a person being raised by a single parent because the parents hated each other and the marriage wasn't healthy. I don't want my sons to think that it's ok for a man to do this to a woman.

Let's Pray:

Lord in the name of Jesus I ask You to help this Princess to not care about what anyone else says or thinks about her or her husband because it only matters what You say. Father, give her ears to hear You clearly on whether she is to stay or go. Help her to be still in the middle of the chaos knowing that You are God and You have all power in Your hand. Help her to seek godly counsel and not feel pressured by anyone to make quick decisions that will change her life. Help her to stay focused on You and not the things and people that are being sent to distract her. Give her a scripture to stand on while she waits on You in Jesus' name, Amen.

Are you in a marriage, relationship, job that you are trying to make a decision on if you should stay or go? Write a prayer asking God for direction on what He wants you to do so you don't make a move when you're to be still.

_____

_____

_____

_____

_____

_____

_____

_____

_____

_____

_____

_____

_____

My reality had been fractured by his actions! I felt foolish for still being in love him but my mind was wanting to stay to see what God was going to do with this hot mess that was our marriage; how was God going to turn this around for His glory and my good but my heart was telling me to run away as fast as I can because I can't handle another painful experience with this man that is supposed to love me. Not making excuses for him but I knew there had to be something wrong within him that would cause him to act out like this (I guess that was my curiosity of why people act the way they do coming out even in this hurtful place in my life) I also know that when he drank the alcohol changed him drastically. Alvin and I talked and prayed together every day as we traveled to work to get direction and understanding on how to move forward. There were so many days that I would be at work and something would trigger me to think about what had happen and I would call Alvin and just scream and holler at him. He would just take it, he wouldn't say anything and when he did say something it was an apology or he would ask me what triggered me. Alvin told me that he thought I was going to get revenge by cheating on him. That upset me because that is not the type of person I am and the fact he thought that made me think he didn't even know me. What I did do is I went out to lunch with my ex. He had come to town for a work convention and prior to him coming he asked me if I would meet him for lunch. I told him yes and I also told Alvin about it. Alvin thought he was coming with me to have lunch and I told him no, that I was going alone. I hadn't seen this man in over 25 years he was also married. I went and got my nails and hair done when I left the house I knew I looked good and so did my husband. We met for lunch at a Firehouse Subs sat there and talked and caught up with life and that was it. I told Alvin I would never inflict the kind of pain that I am feeling unto another woman and there's no man worth me going to hell for.

God opened doors for Alvin to get another position after a couple of months out of work that was in an area that I had some patients in and I made my presence fully known at the facility. Not in an insecure wife kind of way but as a wife who loves her husband and was just dropping by to bring him lunch kind of way. I befriended one of the older ladies that worked with my husband and she kept the women away from him and out of the kitchen. Having Sheila as my prayer partner was and still is priceless to me, she is truly God sent. She helps me to stay prayerful and focused on God, not my husband. Sitting around always wondering what he is doing will drive me crazy.

Let's Pray:

Father in the name of Jesus I ask You to give this Princess a faithful and prayerful prayer partner to cover her and her family in prayer. Teach her how to trust You with her husband and their marriage. Show her husband how to love her and build up her trust in him where it's been shattered. You are the God of reconciliation and recovery. Time heals nothing but You Lord heal all things. Do it for them Lord in the name of Jesus, Amen.

Do you trust God with your husband, children, money, life, and everything else? Pray and think about that question before you answer it. Allow God to show you the people and things you need more trust in Him with. Write a prayer asking God to give you more faith in the areas He reveals to you that your faith needs to be stretched in Him.

_____

_____

_____

_____

_____

_____

_____

_____

_____

Alvin and I continued to work on our marriage day by day. We make it a point to reach out to during the day just to say I was thinking about you or I love you. We ask each other regularly "how's your love tank?" That helps us be mindful of each other's needs. Then our pillow talk changed. It went from focusing a majority of our time on the boys to focusing on each other and making sure each other's mental, emotional, physical, and spiritual needs are met. We started dating each other again and remembering why we fell in love years ago. It's so hard to keep a marriage healthy especially when you have children because the kids take so much time and energy. That's why you have to intentionally stay in love and attracted to your husband. Make him feel and know that you need, want and desire him.

We began getting stronger and God seemed to start sending more and more women my way that were having marital problems. I started questioning God about it because I was still struggling with my pain from it all even though I had chosen to stay and work through it. Every time I would question it I would hear "the things you go through aren't for you they are for the person I send to you to help through it." I have always felt that unless you go through something first hand you will not fully be able to help someone else through it. Who wants someone giving them advice about something they haven't experienced for themselves? Not me. Please don't get me wrong I know we all can have empathy and apathy toward someone's situation but when you experience it for yourself it gives you a different kind of understanding.

On November 8th, 2015 my family was at church when I received a message from a high school classmate telling me to give her a call ASAP along with her phone number. I had no idea why she would be contacting me so I stepped outside and called her. She told me that the man responsible for my mother's death had died. I started crying. I couldn't understand why I was crying for this man and then the Lord let me know that my reaction was the love of Christ in me for him and his family. She went on to say that his house burned down and his body was found in the home on the couch next to the door. I was very sad for him and his family. What a horrible way to die. I wanted to go to the funeral service to be of support to his family but I wasn't able to make it. His death was a closed sealed chapter in my life.

Let's Pray:

Lord, I ask You to fill this Princess with the love of Christ to help her to love the unlovable and to have empathy for other's who hurt. Give Your Princess a heart that is quick to forgive and easy to love. Let her see Your characteristics in others and in herself and teach her how to love with the love of Christ so that people will be drawn to You through her in Jesus' name, Amen.

Is there someone in your life that you want nothing to do with? You know that person that when you hear their name something inside of you flips. Write a prayer for that person asking God to help them be the person God has called them to be.

_____

_____

_____

_____

_____

_____

_____

_____

_____

_____

_____

_____

_____

2016-2017

May of 2016 our 3rd son Isaiah graduated high school and was recruited to play football on a full scholarship to Eastern Arizona. I was not happy about his decision to go so far away from home but I knew I would have to let go of the reigns at some point. I also was very thankful that God provided a full scholarship which helped us save money. Before Isaiah left we sat him down and gave him a repeat of all we had taught him through the years of being a good honest person and Godly man. We also talked to him about girls and to leave them alone. We also told him that he better not bring home a baby and I gave him a bunch of condoms. As much as I prayed and wished my sons would be virgins until marriage I have also been aware enough to know that is a difficult thing for teenagers now days. Not saying it's impossible but it's a very sexual world now days. I had to trust God with him and know that we raised him right.

Let's Pray:

Father in the name of Jesus I come to You. I lift up every Princess that has to let her child go away for college. Encamp Your heavenly angels all around the child to have charge over them and I plead the blood of Jesus over every child that they would be safe from all hurt harm and danger. I pray that the child will make wise decisions and know who is for them and who is against them. Give the child and the Princess discernment so they won't be surprised by foolishness. I ask You, Lord, to keep the lines of communication open between the Princess and her child that the relationship continues to grow and mature in Jesus' name, Amen.

If you have a child/children write a prayer covering them, their school and the other children around them. If you don't have children write a prayer for your nieces/nephews, cousins, godchildren etc.

_____

_____

_____

_____

_____

_____

_____

_____

_____

_____

_____

_____

Alvin had been looking for a home for us to buy since before we moved to Atlanta. I would look every now and then with him but it would tire me out. He continually looked and once we had even contacted a mortgage company sent in all the paperwork and got denied for one thing or another. But this year was our year! We got our credit straight and we applied for a mortgage loan again. We spoke to the loan officers and told them that we wanted to go for the 100% VA Home Loan. Let me give you a quick background: Alvin was in the Army for 7 years he was discharged and his DD-214 states Other than Honorable discharge. That means he is unable to get certain benefits that veterans usually receive. So the loan officer told us that they had never seen someone with this DD-214 discharge get approved for a 100% VA Home Loan. Alvin and I would tell her that we were praying and trusting God and we needed her to do the same. Every week she would contact us letting us know that she had not heard anything yet and wanting to know if we wanted to go ahead and try for a FHA loan. We would tell her no; we know what God promised us and no matter what it looks like we trust Him. Alvin and I prayed every day together we even fasted together trusting God. Of course I also had the Powerful Praying Princesses touching and agreeing in prayer with us for the 100% VA Home Loan. I was at work about at the bedside of a patient that was transitioning into heaven when my husband called me. I couldn't answer the phone because of the sensitivity of the moment so I ignored it and he called back again I did one of those instant text saying I would call right back just to let him know I was busy. He sent me a text back saying "it's ours". At that time my mind was not thinking of the VA loan. After I left the home I called him on the way to my car and he said "we got the 100% VA Loan God did it"! I wanted to hear it from the mortgage people first hand myself so I called her and asked her what was going on. She told me "yes Mrs. Isaac you got it." I started praising God on the phone with her and she said "I have never seen anything like this before." Here's what I knew but hadn't seen happen in our marriage until now: When you and your husband are walking together in agreeance serving God, fasting and praying together and when the head of the house gets his mind, attitude, priorities and life aligned with God's will everything falls in to place! Yes of course trials, tests, and life happens but when things come up my husband and I join faith together as a united front and it makes a world of a difference now.

Let's Pray:

Lord, I lift up the marriage of this Princess and I ask You Lord to restore the trust between her and her husband. Touch her husband's heart that he is able to allow You to lead him as he leads his family. Give him ears to hear and a heart to receive

Your instructions in Jesus' name. I thank You Father that this Princess and her husband are fasting and praying together and standing on Your word as a united front. Lord, raise her husband up to be the spiritual head of the house and show them how to walk in agreeance in Jesus' name, Amen.

In what areas are you lacking trust in your husband? Write a prayer asking God to build the trust in those areas for you towards your husband.

_____

_____

_____

_____

_____

_____

_____

_____

_____

_____

_____

_____

_____

_____

Alvin found a realtor that helped him find our house. Make sure you are prayerful even when it comes to finding the right realtor because they are out to get that commission check and the higher the price of your home the more their check is so make sure they are truly for you. Our realtor knew we wanted our house and she kept saying that she was fighting for us to get it but God let me know that she was lying and was trying to get a bigger commission. One morning I called her and told her we didn't want the house anymore because the price kept going up so let the other people that were supposedly bidding against us have the home. She changed her story so fast and we got the home. I still think we could have gotten it for less but my husband wouldn't let me fire the realtor. Either way I love our beautiful home and we moved into it November of 2016. Sometimes I still look at it and can't believe it's ours. We went from living in a raggedy trailer, losing a home to foreclosure, to now living in a beautiful home. God is a restorer. I even have a Princess wall in our bedroom. It's a wall that I have decorated with princess things, mirrors, and my pictures with me in my crown or tiara. Alvin bought me a tiara for my birthday this year and I know it was God that told him to buy it because I really wanted one but I didn't tell him. It made me cry when he gave it to me because I knew he was hearing from the Lord. I wear it sometimes when I clean the house or if I'm not feeling like the Princess I am I'll put it on to remind me that I am God's Powerful Praying Princess.

Ever since my mother and grandmother died Christmas time has been very hard for me. I didn't like putting up decorations or trees and I disliked Christmas music. But moving into our new home along with Alvin and me working on our new relationship changed something in me. I told Alvin I wanted to decorate the new house for Christmas so I bought all purple and silver decorations and went crazy decorating the entire house inside and out. My husband even bought some purple decorations for me (he usually won't buy me purple anymore because I own so many purple things but I think he was just happy that I rekindled my love of Christmas again). For Christmas Alvin bought me a new wedding ring something I had been telling him I wanted for several years he finally got it. We talked in January or 2017 about renewing our vows for our 20th anniversary and decided that our back yard would be the perfect place. I called my friend Tara (the events planner for everyone and everything) and told her what we wanted to do and she ran with it and the planning began. Because Alvin and I didn't have a wedding ceremony when we got married in 1997 at the courthouse we wanted the renewal to be a wedding ceremony. I called my sister cousins Marquita, Linda, and Angel to let them know I wanted them to stand with me as my bridesmaids. Alvin started contacting the men he wanted here by his side and he also had our sons as his groom's men. June 2017 we had our 20th vow renewal and it was perfect! Friends and family came from far and near to celebrate with us. My mentor Pastor Mike came from Florida to officiate it, a friend of my husbands he hadn't seen in 20 plus years came from Texas, Alvin's family came from Florida, New Jersey, and Pennsylvania and all my sister cousins were the only family on my side that came and that was fine with me. Isaiah had brought his girlfriend from Arizona home for the summer so she was there too and we all had a great time.

Both Alvin and I started new jobs at the end of June which was wonderful financially and life seemed to be going good for a while. But different things began to trigger me and the trust-building Alvin and I had been working on. It was like one day I woke up and the fear of my husband cheating on me came flooding back with a vengeance and my relationship with God also was suffering. I don't know if it was Alvin getting a new job and moving to a different building that wasn't as easy for me to pop up and visit as the old one or what it was. Alvin and I continued to pray together every morning and talk but memories of the pain kept creeping into my mind and dreams. I couldn't understand why after several months of peace and relationship building with Alvin, I was feeling like it all just happened. Alvin was confused too not understanding how it seemed we had come so far to just be right back where we started. We prayed more and my prayer partner Sheila prayed with me and for me. I know that the enemy comes to steal, kill, and destroy and he (the enemy) was angry that we decided to fight for our marriage. I had to learn how to bind up my fears and allow God to help me see myself as beautiful, intelligent, and worthy of love. Alvin has really shown me that he cares that he hurt me and not just tells me he loves me but shows me he loves me every day.

Let's Pray:

Lord, I ask You to mute the mouth of the enemy that comes to steal, kill, and destroy the life of Your Princess. Father, help her to stand on Your promises and read Your word. Lord, teach her how to think about the things that are true, right, pure, lovely and praiseworthy in You. Teach her how to get control over her thoughts and perceptions in Jesus name. Lord, I thank You that she is made whole in You. I thank You that she is the apple of Your eye. I thank You that her marriage is strong and that her husband loves her the way Christ loves the church. Father, I thank You that her husband only has eyes for her in Jesus' name, Amen.

Have you been cheated on by your husband or someone you were dating and now you are insecure and the enemy keeps whispering lies in your ear? Write a prayer of thanksgiving to God for everything you are and your husband is to you.

_____

_____

_____

_____

_____

_____

_____

_____

_____

_____

_____

_____

_____

Thanksgiving of 2017 Isaiah brought his girlfriend home with him again for the holiday. The boys all went to Florida for Thanksgiving and Alvin and I stayed home for Thanksgiving and invited some friends over for dinner because I was on-call for the hospital. For Christmas this year Alvin bought me a 23 and Me DNA kit. I was so excited because I had wanted to know what my ancestry was made up of because if Anthony is my biological father there has to be Mexican in my DNA. Dad's mother my grandmother was Mexican and African American. I sent the kit off and waited the 2 long months it took to get my results. I was so nervous when I got the results and went through the list of 36 different ethnicities amazed at the mixture of it all but really only searching for any evidence of my "Hispanic" heritage. There was nothing that I recognized as Latino or Hispanic. To say the least I was upset because I felt like I was going to continue my search to find my biological father. Since starting this book I have been doing more research and I found out that genetic testing can't tell whether or not a person is Hispanic or Latino because Hispanics typically have the mixture of European, African, Native American and sometimes East Asian, Iberian, and Portuguese. I have all of these and more! Of course I would still love to do a sibling DNA test on my brother and sister that I know for sure are my dad's biological children just to know 100% that I am dad's child. One day I'll have it done (I'll keep you all posted).

2018

January on a Wednesday evening Christian, Ezekiel and I were getting ready to go to bible study at the church and I got a phone call from Alvin. He was on his way home from work and told me he wanted me to wait at the house for him because he had to talk to me. I asked him why he couldn't talk to me on the phone because I don't like being late. He stated that it was something we needed to talk about face to face. I kept trying to get him to just tell me but he wouldn't and wanted me to wait home for him. The boys and I were sitting in the truck waiting on him when he got home so he could just get in the truck with us and we could leave and talk on the way to church. But he says to me to come in the house so we can talk by this time I'm not happy because we're going to be late to church. My mind is racing trying to think of what he needed to talk to me about then he says "Do you remember the dream I had about the fish?" At this point I am not trying to remember any dreams I just want him to tell me what he needs to tell me! He finally says "Isaiah is pregnant. Alexis and Isaiah are pregnant." I don't remember what all I said but it went something like this: I told that boy not to do this I gave him condoms and I put money in his account to make sure he could buy them if needed. I told him not to trust anybody. I'm gonna kick his butt! I wanted to know why Isaiah called my husband and told him but didn't call and tell me. Alvin said to me "that's why I told him not to call you because I knew you were going to be mad and you might say something you may regret to him." Even though I was upset I was glad Alvin did tell me the news that we were going to be grandparents. I called Isaiah and I did let him know I wasn't happy about the situation but that we were going to support him, Alexis and the baby in every way we could. It took me a while to get use to the idea of being a grandmother but once I got over the sting of it I was okay. I also thought about my past: I had 4 sons by 3 different men so who am I to judge. Yes I taught him better but as a mom I had to remember he is going to live his life just like we all do. I had to remember every one of my children has a life to live and even though I want to protect them from the pains and disappointments of life I can't because that's part of their testimony and learning.

Let's Pray:

Gracious and Heavenly Father I come to You asking You to cover ever Princess that is a mother. Give her the comfort in knowing that You have a plan for her children and a purpose. Father show her what to pray and how to pray for her children that when they do make mistakes in their lives she will be able to talk to them in understanding knowing that every decision she made in her life wasn't perfect. Help us to extend grace to our children along with wise words to help them see their mistakes and learn from them. Help us be better parents to our children then our parents were to us. Father, help our children to be better parents to their children than we are to them in Jesus' name, Amen.

Are your children making what you consider to be bad decisions? Write a prayer for them to be led by God and protected by His angels to walk in the purpose God has created them to complete.

_____

_____

_____

_____

_____

_____

_____

_____

_____

_____

_____

_____

March of 2018 I walked across the stage and received my BA in Psychology. I was so happy it took me years to get it because life happens but I did it. I have always been curious of why people do the things they do and what in their upbringing causes them to respond or think the way they do. Also I and 5 other women in my church made church history by being the first class of ordained Elders at Global Impact Christian Ministries. In May Alvin and I flew out to Arizona for Isaiah and Alexis's graduation from Eastern Arizona with their Associates Degrees I was so proud of both of them. Alvin, Isaiah, Alexis and I drove from Arizona to Atlanta after graduation to move Isaiah back home. That was the longest ride I have ever taken and can't imagine ever doing it again. I like to fly so I can get to my destination quickly and if I do drive I like to drive straight through.

At the beginning of June Davian moved out of our home and in with his girlfriend Amanda who is in college in Alabama. We had been trying to communicate and allow him to stay at home ever since he quit college but he couldn't seem to follow our very simple rules which were talking to us and giving us $100 a month. I protected him as long as I could with Alvin but I finally had to let go and support my husband in doing what needed to be done to help Davian grow up. We gave him a move out date but we told him we would continue to pay his cellphone bill and car insurance until he was able to do it for himself (he is also on our health insurance). Supporting my husband in putting our son out of the house was one of the hardest things I had to ever do. I am a momma bear and will do anything for my sons so to have to agree with my husband on this was very hard on me.

Let's Pray:

Father in the name of Jesus I come to You asking You to touch this Princess when it comes to making a tough decision that will help her children grow. Help her to be at peace with not intervening in their growth process. Teach her how to pray for her adult children and how to let the father in the son's life teach that son how to be a man. Show this Princess how to take a supporting role in her adult child's life now and pray, pray, in Jesus' name, Amen.

Do you and your husband see eye to eye when it comes to raising the kids? Are you co-parenting well with your child's other parent (s)? Write a prayer asking God to help all parents involved with your children to parent together in peace and unity.

_____

_____

_____

_____

_____

_____

_____

_____

_____

_____

_____

That month we also did a pregnancy photoshoot, a gender reveal-baby shower and Isaiah also surprised Alexis with a wedding proposal. Alexis's whole family traveled from the Native American reservation in Arizona to our home in Atlanta where they all stayed. My husband couldn't understand why I went a little over board for them but I let him know I didn't have a baby shower for any of my children and it was something I always wanted. I wasn't celebrating them having a child out of wedlock but I wanted to celebrate the life of my first grandchild and have wonderful memories to share. Alexis went back to Arizona to have the baby and the day after the birth in August Isaiah and I flew out to Arizona to be with Alexis and Isaiah Jr.

my beautiful grandson. As a new grandmother I haven't agreed on everything my son and his fiancé did in their relationship but again that's a place I will continue to grow and mature. I pray a lot and keep quiet unless I'm asked my opinion and it's not easy.

Let's Pray:

Lord, I come to You lifting up Your daughter asking You to give her comfort and peace in knowing that she has raised her children to be respectful and wise adults. Help her to keep the doors of her relationships open with her children that they know she is available for them when they need to talk and want a listening ear. Help her to speak in wisdom and stay prayerful. Help Your Princess to know that her words have power so she needs to use them wisely in Jesus' name, Amen.

How is your relationship with your children? Write a prayer for your relationship. If you don't have children then write a prayer for someone else's relationship with their children.

_____

_____

_____

_____

_____

_____

_____

_____

_____

_____

_____

_____

_____

Also in August, the Director of Spiritual Care (full-time Chaplain) resigned his position at Piedmont Henry Hospital where I had been volunteering at for years before they hired me as a PRN On-Call Chaplain. In 2011 God promised me that I would be the Director of Spiritual Care there at some point so when he resigned I applied for the position and was interviewed a couple of months later. On the same day of my interview, my Aunt Terry died and Marquita asked me to do the Eulogy. At first, I didn't think I would be able to do it because she was like another mother to me but I prayed and the Lord showed me what to say. Aunt Terry was a hot mess but one thing I had seen her do at every funeral in the past few years was to raise her hand whenever the preacher would extend salvation to the congregation. I had also talked to her on a couple of occasions about accepting Jesus and she did. My family as a whole has never been "religious" church-going people and the first time I went home after getting saved my family members would run from me and say things like "hide the beer here comes the preacher." So to preach at my aunt's funeral was a scary thing for me. When I began to talk to my family the Lord led me to talk about how Aunt Terry knew that the only way to heaven was to accept Jesus Christ. I also shared how she would raise her hand to accept Jesus at every funeral when the pastor gave the invitation to Christ. I went on to say that even though she didn't live the "Christian Life" she accepted Jesus and that's what God wants for all of us. No matter what we have done in our lives Jesus's grace is sufficient. I also told them Jesus would have died on that cross even if you were the only person on earth. I refreshed their memory about my life and the sins I committed and when I extended salvation so many of my family members accepted Jesus I couldn't even count them all because my eyes were full of tears.

The whole process of hiring for the hospital was ridiculously long but it was all worth it when I got the phone call on Nov. 2, 2018, telling me that I had been chosen as the new Full-time Chaplain. It took 7 years for God's promise to manifest but I didn't stop believing it would and it did! This is just the beginning of my dream vocation. My dream vocation is to be a Chaplain Supervisor that means I want to train people how to be a Chaplain.

Not even a month after I got home from that funeral on Nov. 22nd my Aunt Joy was 88 when she (my mom's aunt) died and then on Dec.16th my 90-year-old Aunt Velma died (my mom's Uncle Allan's wife). I was unable to make it home for their funerals but my heart was so heavy for my family. Aunt Joy was a firecracker and so much fun to be around. Aunt Velma was the first consistent Christian in my life; she was always sweet and soft-spoken but strong and courageous.

2019

January 1, 2019, I got a phone call from my sister- cousin Linda telling me that our cousin Marsha (Sharon's sister and Aunt Velma's daughter) had died. My heart ached because Aunt Velma had just died and Marsha had been her caregiver. Marsha had taken care of both of her parents until they died neglecting her own health. One of Marsha's daughters asked me if I would do the eulogy for her mother's memorial service. At the time I hadn't planned on going home because my finances weren't looking too good but she told me that there was no one else she wanted to do the services and that she would pay for me to get home to Emporia (and our church helped with gas too). I couldn't say no to her.

Honestly, I had no idea what to say for her eulogy either because although I loved Marsha I hadn't been very close to her but God gave me the words for her funeral too. During every funeral I have ever officiated I talk about forgiveness and not dying with any un-forgiveness in your heart. Now although I had forgiven my uncle years ago I had not spoken to him and we had been in the same room many times but I completely ignored him like he was invisible. While talking about forgiveness during Marsha's funeral I felt a tugging on my heart telling I needed to be an example of that forgiveness to my uncle and others in my family by going up to him as I was telling my family bye and telling him bye as well. I didn't know how I felt about it but I know God is moved by obedience, not our feelings. Please don't get me wrong I'm not telling anyone to talk to their abuser but what I am saying is be obedient to what God tells you in His word and in your prayer time.

Let's Pray:

Father in the name of Jesus I lift up every Princess that has had a lot of death in her family. Help her and her family have peace in the midst of their grief process. Lord, if she ever has to speak at a funeral or does an eulogy give her the words to speak with confidence and love. Show her how to pray for her family and give her the gift of forgiveness to others. Lord, if she has been abused in any kind of way help her to forgive her abusers out of obedience to Your word in Jesus' name, Amen.

Have you had a family member die that you or your family is still struggling with the grief? Write a prayer for you and your family for God to mend your broken hearts.

_____

_____

_____

_____

_____

_____

_____

_____

_____

_____

_____

_____

_____

Throughout this year the Lord has been teaching me that I must continually extend grace to others even when I want to say harsh words to people who in my opinion really deserve a good cussing. I have to bite my tongue (even if my mouth is full of blood), humble myself and answer with a gentle word because it turns away wrath (Proverbs 15). Even when someone is picking on my child (adult child) and I want to get in the boxing ring for him (God is still working on me). I have to stand back and fight differently through praying for his situation. I understand that I have a new role in my son's lives because all of them are considered grown (even though they will always be my babies).

Ezekiel graduated high school this year and on the same weekend Isaiah and Alexis got married (I am so happy about this). They decided on a Thursday that they wanted to get married on Sunday and praise God it all worked out. It's such a blessing that Alvin and I have raised 4 young men who all graduated high school and are now living productive lives. Christian is living at home and still being Christian he brings so much joy, laughter and love to our family I thank God for him every day. Davian is still living in Alabama, he and Amanda (who I love, love, love) are doing well. He has his own path to walk and I may not be happy with all of his decisions but I have to trust we raised him right and God's got him. Isaiah, Alexis, and the baby all live with us (I love it). We switched the upstairs of our home into their own living space and let them know they can stay as long as they need and want. Both of them will be returning to college this fall and I've already found a babysitter for Jr. Ezekiel is starting college in August studying to be an EMT and then onto the Fire Academy to be a fireman.

In whatever my sons want to do in life I know my role is to pray for God's will to be done no matter what. Alvin and I are best friends now. We talk about everything and when something is bothering us, we discuss it. There are no holding things in for an extended amount of time. We take to heart Ephesians 4:26 "In your anger do not sin": Do not let the sun go down while you are still angry." No marriage or person is perfect but we are two imperfect people willing to continue to work on our marriage together. Every day he shows me I can trust him and he has been sober now for 4 years. I too stopped having an occasional glass of wine 4 years ago in support of Alvin not drinking. Of course, we still get on each other's nerves sometimes but we are in this marriage till death do us part. I have set up family counseling sessions for Alvin, the boys, Alexis, Amanda and I so we can discuss the book's contents and have a safe place for everyone to voice their concerns, anger, hurt, etc. I'm still striving to get closer to the Lord. I trust Him more and more every day and I know I need Him.

While waiting to publish this book my Aunt Linda Rose died on July 19, 2019. She was my safe place when I was growing up. I tried every weekend and the whole summer to stay at her house. I knew no one would hurt me at her house and we always had fun there. My husband and I made it to Emporia for her funeral as well. I have never been home so much in a year before since I moved away 23 years ago. This visit although was for another funeral was one of the better visits for me. Alvin and I went and picked up my 80-year-old Aunt Sarah the last living sibling of my grandmother's. We spent the day with her running errands she needed to get done, went out to eat and hung out with other family members. I am so glad we took the time to spend quality time with her.

I never thought anyone would be interested in hearing about me. I never really thought my life was hard I guess because I didn't have a choice of whether or not to live it. God made that decision for me when he formed me in my mother's womb. I used to always ask God why He gave me the crazy dysfunctional family I grew up in but now I just say thank You Lord for my family. We may have issues but what family doesn't? Because of my family, I am a better wife, mother, grandmother, Christian, friend, and Chaplain. I have learned so much from my life experiences and those life experiences help me to relate to so many different people especially in my profession. I listen to and support patients and families through some of the most critical times in their lives with sickness and death. I talk to and pray with people at church, in the grocery stores, at gas stations, anywhere God has me to help someone who is hurting. I've learned to be open and willing to listen, hear, and help even when it seems inconvenient. I desire to be the answer to someone else's prayer.

One thing God has shown me and is continuing to show me in life is that there is no relationship that He can't bring reconciliation to. The people involved in the relationship have to have a forgiving heart and a willing mind. Is it easy? No. Is it possible? Yes. Is it worth it? Oh yes. Not all relationships will be reconciled and that's okay but all people do need to be forgiven even if you no longer communicate with them. Don't let anyone have that much power over you that you don't forgive. Life can change in an instant and is too short to stay mad and full of resentment towards anyone. I see people die almost every day and there are so many unspoken words family members regret not saying. Do I have a relationship with everyone I have forgiven? No. That doesn't mean I hate them or hold any unforgiveness towards them it just means I know who my friends are and who my foes are and I won't waste my energy on my foes but I do pray for them. One of the best memes I've seen on Facebook said something like this "You know you have matured when you're able to sit at the table with your Judas." That blessed and freed me because I have been in situations where I have had dinner with a group of people and not everyone at that table was for me. Even though I knew a few of them could care less about me I still enjoyed my meal and the other people at the table. I always remember that with God for me who can be against me? I have come to realized that my hardest critic is myself. I hold myself to a very high standard and I use to feel like I had to be perfect. There is no way I can be perfect but I know that I am perfectly flawed and perfectly Tynika. I have learned and am still learning to forgive myself for the mistakes I have made and are making in being a daughter, mother, friend, wife, cousin, sister, and person. There are so many times I say something and immediately I regret saying it. I have a crazy sense of humor and I have prayed to ask God to change it but it hasn't changed yet! In my profession, my sense of humor could be seen as inappropriate at times and I struggle with saying what comes to mind and not filtering it before I say it. You can see where it can get me in trouble sometimes! So I continually repent! I know the only perfect being that never made a mistake is Jesus so please forgive yourself so you can free yourself from the stress of perfection because we as human beings are flawed but we are FORGIVEN.

There's so much more I could have written about my life but I wanted to be obedient to what I felt I was being directed to write by the Lord. I pray that something in my life helped you realize you're not alone.

Have you forgiven yourself for mistakes and bad decisions you have made? What are you blaming yourself for that you need to let go of? If you need to forgive yourself write a letter of forgiveness to yourself.

_____

_____

_____

_____

_____

_____

_____

_____

_____

_____

_____

_____

_____

I love teaching people about prayer also praying with and for people. I pray this next section of my book helps you get more comfortable in prayer and understanding it's our right and privilege as children of God to communicate with our Heavenly Father. It's not hard, just talk to Him like you talk to everyone else but remember He already knows all your business so you might as well be transparent and honest with Him.

What is prayer?

What is prayer? Prayer is our lifeline to God. It's communicating to our Father. It's also listening to God and waiting for instruction. I have been on several prayer ministries in churches before birthing the Powerful Praying Princesses. During this time I have prayed with and prayed for many people and a lot of the people I have encountered have said to me that they don't know how to pray or if they do pray they can't pray for an hour. I explain to them that all prayer is, is talking to God, having a conversation with Him. Yes, it's a conversation and yes God is still speaking to His children. The question is: Are we listening? Prayer is about the relationship with our Heavenly Father. People get frustrated in praying because they don't see instant results, they lose faith. They don't understand that they have the authority through Jesus Christ to get their prayers answered themselves. They just have to use and stretch their faith in God. Some Christians pray as an act of a religious exercise that's done because that's what Christians are supposed to do. Again it's about the relationship with our Father, staying in continuous communication with Him.

How do we approach God in prayer?

Dr. Myles Munroe in his book "Prayer" says (p. 65) "We must learn to enter God's presence with the right spirit, approach, and preparation so we can commune with Him and offer effective prayers as God's priests." When I go to God in prayer I always start by telling Him how awesome He is to me and just glorifying Him for being the God of my life. I also tell Him how much I love and adore Him just for being my Father. It helps me to set the atmosphere when I praise the Lord during my prayer time so I also love to play worship music.

The Lord's Prayer

The Lord's Prayer in Matthew 6:9-13 is not a ritual prayer, but it is an example of a prayer to model our prayers after. The Lord's Prayer opens up with worship, an acknowledgment of who God is. We have to reverence God in our worship; we must be in awe of the great mercy, grace, and holiness of God that allows us to honor Him. This is not a prayer of request but God declares that He is faithful to do what He said He would do. The Lord outlines the steps into prayer.

Step 1 is the acknowledgment of who God is by saying "Our Father which art in heaven Hallowed (made holy, consecrated) be thy name." That's opening prayer up in worship unto our holy God; we are telling God that we know He is the creator and ruler of the universe. He is El HaKadosh (The Holy God) and Elohim (God our Creator).

Step 2 is the acknowledgment of God's Kingdom and God's Will "thy Kingdom come thy will be done in earth as it is in heaven" this is a request that God's Kingdom and Will be activated here in the earth. We also have to realize and accept that God's Will for our lives is better than our own will. We are to be praying and seeking the heart and mind of God then our will for our lives will be the same as God's Will for us.

Step 3 is the application of God's Word, Jesus says, "Give us this day our daily bread." We must eat/read the Word of God daily and pray the Word.

Step 4 is repentance unto God, "And forgives us our debts, as we forgive our debtors," we have to have a repentant heart when coming to God. Jesus is showing us that we need to forgive others that have hurt us or done us wrong the same way God forgives us for our wrongdoings.

Step 5 is the attentiveness to the work of God "and lead us not into temptation but deliver us from evil." We are asking God to lead us and to keep us from stumbling into traps set by the enemy and the attacks of the enemy.

Step 6 is an affirmation of God in everything we do; "For thine is the kingdom, and the power, and the glory, forever." Jesus is affirming that God is eternal (El Olam) and powerful.

Step 7 is sealing the prayer with God. Jesus ends the prayer with "Amen" which means so be it. It is done. He didn't end it within Jesus, amen but Jesus does tell us in John 15:16, "ask the Father in my name and He shall give it to you."

What gives us the right to pray?

God originally gave us the right to commune with Him when He first created Adam to have dominion over the earth. Then God would walk and talk with Adam in the Garden of Eden. When Adam sinned, forfeiting our dominion authority, Satan became the god of this world and not man (2Corinthians 4:4). This action left humans estranged from God, feeling isolated, unsure of our relationship with God and our purpose in life. Also when this happened it made God give man free will, leaving it up to us to choose whether or not we want a relationship with God. Jesus is the "Second Adam." God's Word had to become flesh for mankind. Restoring mankind would have been impossible if not for Jesus Christ. Jesus had to be sinless and He had to choose to do the Will of God, that's the only way God could redeem humanity. Jesus Christ being born from a virgin, living as a righteous sinless man, dying on the cross and rising from the dead gives us the right to pray! Jesus was the walking, talking, Word of God who restored to us the authority. Praise God!!!

Praying in Jesus name

John 14:13-14 says "I will do anything you ask the Father in my name so that the Father will be given glory because of the Son. If you ask me to do something I will do it." This does not mean that we can just pray anything and just because we put "in the name of Jesus" at the end of it that God will give it to us. That is unbiblical. When we pray in the name of Jesus it means praying with His authority and asking God the Father to act upon our prayers because we come in the name of His Son, Jesus. Praying in Jesus' name we are praying for things that will honor and glorify Jesus. This gives us the confidence in approaching God that if we ask anything according to His will

He hears us and will answer our prayers (I John 5:14-15).

You have to have FAITH

I believe to have faith is to believe in something or someone, to fully trust, to be so confident that you base your actions on what you believe. To have faith is to be fully convinced of the truthfulness and reliability of what you believe in. Faith in God is a response to God's Word which moves God to act. Faith is a spiritual substance. When you have this substance in you, it communicates to you a certain inner knowing that the thing you are hoping for is established, even before you see any material evidence that it has happened. Faith in God must be from the heart. Romans 10:10 (NIV) says, "For it is with your heart that you believe and are justified, and it is with your mouth that you profess your faith, and are saved." Hebrews 11:6 says "Without faith we can't please God." Kenneth Hagin in his book, Foundations for Faith (p.5), says "Faith is grasping the unrealities of hope and bringing them into the realm of reality." In Hebrews 11:1 the Apostle Paul tells us, "Now faith is the substance of things hoped for the evidence of things not seen." Throughout the 11th chapter of Hebrews, we are given examples of the "People of Faith" that are in the Bible. By faith, Abraham offered his son Isaac to God because Abraham had faith in God that he knew God would provide a sacrifice even if it would have been Isaac. Thank God He provided a ram in the bush. Faith led Moses' parents to hide him for three months and put him in a basket in the river. Moses grew up and his faith led him to refuse to be known as the son of Pharaoh's daughter. Instead (Hebrews 11) he chose to suffer with God's people and God used him to lead the Israelites into the "Promise Land." There are so many examples of great and awesome things God can and will do when we as believers have faith in Him and pray believing God can and will do what He says He will do. I understand it is sometimes hard to have the faith we should have in God. There have been many times I have asked God why haven't I received what I have been praying for myself, but someone I have interceded for or agreed with, in prayer received their request quickly. I a lot of the time would have more faith for someone else to receive their need then I had for my own need to be met. I had to check my own faith and relationship with God for myself and pray to ask God to increase my faith in Him. Also being an intercessor God continually stretches our faith to get us where we need to be in Him according to the level, He is taking us to. Waiting on God is to trust God and know God is and will move on your behalf. Isaiah 40:31 says "But those who wait on the LORD shall renew their strength; they shall mount up with wings like eagles, they shall run and not be weary, they shall walk and not faint." Some events that have happened in my life that have shaken my faith and have caused me to get weary and faint because I felt I shouldn't have had to go through that issue or that heartache; for example when God revealed to me that my husband had been cheating on me. I for the life of me couldn't understand why me. I was very angry with God and my husband and had a very hard time reconciling both relationships. I thank God for my prayer partner Princess Sheila who prayed for me when I couldn't pray for myself. Every time something would happen to me I would ask God why me and I would hear in my spirit "Why not you?" Look at everything Jesus went through and He was without sin. Why would you not have to go through anything?" Although I don't want to hear that I also know that the things I go through are for me to help others through those same things and after I get through that storm I am more mature and my faith is stronger. Also, it is not always what we go through but the attitude in which we go through it. We have to keep an attitude of faith, praise and gratitude. No it's not easy but it is possible, it is a choice we have to make. I had to say to myself yes I'm hurting but my God is a healer. Yes I'm angry but my God gives me peace. Yes, but God. Yes but God. That has to be our attitude. Is it always easy? Heck no! But with God it is possible.

There are several different types of Prayer:

Prayer of Agreement (Matthew 18:19-20, NIV)

In Matthew 18:19 Jesus tells us that if two or three of us get together in His name and agree about anything God will accept it. That is powerful. We as believers have to understand the authority behind agreement in prayer. God backs up our praying in agreement! I know I have seen God do some awesome things and most of the time it has been when I have touched and agreed in prayer with someone for God to move on my behalf or someone else I'm praying for. I remember one miracle God privileged me to be a part of. It was several years ago. We were having a healing conference at the church and my husband's cousin Kim came up to me asking for prayer. She told me that she was going to have surgery the next day because the doctors had found a 20-ounce size tumor in her abdomen. I looked up and saw two other people God led me to get to touch and agree with in prayer so they could be a part of what He was about to do. I got everyone together and we laid hands on Kim and prayed that God would do the surgery supernaturally and that when she got to the hospital for surgery there would be no tumor. She went to surgery the next morning and when the doctors opened her up there was nothing there but a little bit of scar tissue as if the surgery had already been done!! I'm getting excited just thinking about it.

That miracle built my faith up so much towards God's healing power and a promise that the Lord had told me when I first got saved. He had spoken to me that He had anointed my hands to heal. I had held onto that promise but when that miracle happened I started walking in that authority. I have the faith in God that when He leads me to lay hands on someone and pray for their healing, no matter what it is, He will do it.

Prayer of Petition (Matthew 21:22, NIV)

The prayer of petition is the most common type of prayer. Most Christians learn this type of prayer when they first get saved. This is when we are asking God to do something for us personally. This prayer has to be done in faith just like all other prayers. Perhaps this is the most used and misused type of prayer. We all want material prosperity or to be famous but we have to ask for His will to be done. God is concerned about what concerns us and wants us to come to Him making our request known, but it pleases Him when we ask for the Holy Spirit and to be more like Jesus. When I first got saved I prayed a lot for God to use me and also for God to give me all the spiritual gifts He had, I still pray for that to be done.

A Prayer of Petition:

Father in the name of Jesus I ask You to forgive me for all of my sins. Lord, I am coming to You because You are my refuge, my provider, my strength, my healer and my counselor. I need You,

Lord, to touch my life. I want to be different, changed, and made whole in You. Wash and cleanse me God from the top of my head to the soles of my feet clean me up. Lord, fill me with Your Holy Spirit and give me the spirit of discernment to know who is for me and who is against me. Lord, make me wiser than my enemies that my enemies will not be able to win against me. Lord, I am a faithful tither and Your Word in Malachi 3 says that if I tithe You will pour out blessings and prevent pests from devouring my harvest. Father, I have bills that need to be paid and You said that You are Jehovah Jira my provider please give me peace while You work out the money for my bills. Lord I am Your child and You are the best Father and provider there is and *ever will be. Thank You Lord that with You I am victorious and well taken care of in Jesus mighty name amen.*

Prayer of Consecration (Luke 22:42, NIV)

This prayer is praying that God's will be done. This is us as children of God yielding to the will of God for every situation in our lives having the faith in God that He knows, wants, and will do what is best for us at all times. As God's children, we should be praying to have the mind of Christ and in having the mind of Christ we will know the will of God. Also in the reading of His Word, we find His Will. This is always a part of my prayer time.

A Prayer of Consecration:

Father, I come to You humbly knowing that You are Alpha and Omega. Lord everything I am and need is in You. I yield my life to You God knowing You have the final say so in my life. I give it all to You Lord. I give You my heart, my mind, my talk and my walk, my motives, agendas, my children, my husband, my finances everything is Yours. I need the mind of Christ that I will know how to live my life for You that I may know how to respond to those around me and even have a greater understanding of everything. Give me a good understanding of Your Word when I study and help me to memorize it. Set me apart from those who try to use and abuse me that I will be totally surrendered to You in Jesus' name amen.

Prayer of Praise and Adoration (I Chronicles 29:10-13, NIV)

There are many of these prayers in the Bible and David is the author of most of them. This type of prayer is centered solely on God and His eternal characteristics: His glory, power, faithfulness, beauty, grace, mercy, and love. This is the type of prayer that our personal devotional prayer time should start with. During this time is when the joy of the Lord comes and His perfect peace comes, healing comes, and all other perfect gifts God has for us come in His presence during this time. I love telling God how great and powerful He is. In this time of prayer, I call Him by his powerful names: Alpha,

Omega, El Olam, Jehovah Jirah, Jehovah Nissi, etc. You have to find the names of God that describe the character of God that he is for you in your current situation. I suggest you find a book of the names of God that defines them and gives you scripture to back it up.

A Prayer of Praise and Adoration:

Lord, You are everything I need. You ,God, are Alpha and Omega the Beginning and the End. You are the Author and Finisher of my faith. In You Lord, I find my peace and comfort because You are Jehovah Shalom. Lord, I praise You that You are El Olam my Everlasting God who supplies all of my needs according to Your riches in glory through Christ Jesus. Thank You, Father, that You are Jehovah Ralphe, my Healer. Lord, I bless Your holy and righteous name. I reverence You Lord and I adore Your awesomeness because there is none like You. You are God and Your God all by Yourself in Jesus name I pray amen.

Prayer of Intercession (Romans 8:26-27, 3, 4, NIV)

This is the type of prayer that I believe brings us closer to God's heart. Jesus is in heaven. He is our High Priest and He is interceding for us to the Father. When we pray for others we are like Jesus. This is the type of praying when you have to be prepared to get woke up at all hours of the night to cry out for someone. This is where we lay down our own lives for God in letting go of anything that is not God's Will. There are so many people and situations in this crazy dying world that God wants us interceding in prayer for. Look at the 5 o'clock or 10 o'clock news you'll never run out of people to intercede for. From the very beginning of my walk with Jesus people have asked me to pray for them and I have seen God do some awesome miracles and within the past few years, God has taken me to a deeper level of intercession. You will never know the full plan of God unless you pray and seek Him. You just have to have the faith to jump in!

A Prayer of Intercession:

Father in the name of Jesus I lift up the person reading this book right now and I ask you to place in them a spirit of intercession. Lord give them people and situations to intercede for. Build up their faith in You and give them the discipline to wake up in the midnight hour to cry out on the behalf of someone else. Cover their prayer time with You that they hear You clearly and know Your voice. Help them to be all You have called them to be for Your Kingdom. Give them power and authority that they walk in the fullness of it through Christ Jesus amen.

Prayer of Thanksgiving (Psalm 107:8-9, NIV)

After you have prayed and believe that what you have prayed God is already moving on your behalf, start giving God thanks. Thank Him in advance for answering your prayer. This is where you show God your faith because you haven't seen the manifestation of the prayers yet but you are trusting God that it's already done. God delights in our praises to Him. Give Him the glory for what He is doing and going to do for you.

A Prayer of Thanksgiving:

God, I thank You for dispatching Your angels to work on my behalf. I thank You, Lord, that my marriage is loving, thank You Father that my husband loves me the way Christ loves the church. Thank You, Lord, that my children love You and have a relationship with You in Jesus' name. Father, I bless You that You are my Provider, Healer and Way Maker. You're everything I need and I thank You in Jesus' name amen.

Praying in the Spirit (Ephesians 6:18, NIV)

Praying in the Spirit comes through our spirit, not our minds. The Bible says in Ephesians 6:18 (NIV) "And pray in the Spirit on all occasions with all kinds of prayers and requests. With this in mind, be alert and always keep on praying for all the Lord's people." Paul is telling us in this scripture to pray, pray in every situation in every kind of way we know how to pray. When praying in the Spirit we are being led by the Spirit how to pray and what to pray. Read the word of God, praise God, repent for your sins now listen and start praying. Don't think about what's coming out of your mouth let God use you and you just say it, pray it.

Praying in Tongues (Acts 2:4, NIV)

Part of the evidence of being filled with the Holy Spirit is the evidence of speaking in tongues. It takes faith to pray in tongues. It's a gift from God because it is the Holy Spirit praying through you. Just like all of the gifts of the Spirit not every person will have every gift. Please don't think you're not filled with the Holy Spirit because you aren't speaking in tongues right now. When praying in tongues the devil can't understand what we are praying. I try to pray in tongues for at least 30 minutes to an hour daily. This could be in the morning, in the shower, while driving, although sometimes I may have to pull over on the side of the road and get my praise on.

Please Remember

We have such a privilege as children of God to be able to commune with Him in prayer. We need to take advantage of it and embrace it. We can come boldly to the throne room of God and make our request known to Him and have the confidence in knowing that He will answer our prayers. We have to find His promises to us in His word and remind Him of them when we pray. We have to remember these 4 things:

1. P.U.S.H (pray until something happens) even when you don't feel like it.
2. Much prayer much power, little prayer little power, no prayer no power.

3. BELIEVE Because Emmanuel Lives I Expect Victory Every time ~ Darlene Bishop

4. Please forget the old saying "Don't question God."

How are you supposed to learn if you don't ask any questions? When you were a child didn't you ask your parents questions? You as a parent don't your children ask you questions? The answer is yes to all of the questions. Ask God what you want and need to know. Yes, you can even ask Him "Why", although you may not like the answer but please ask the question.

Here are some prayers I have written over the years. I hope they help you and bless you.

A Prayer of Submission to God

(Job 22:21-22 NIV)

Father in the name of Jesus I come to You humbly exalting You and submitting my heart, mind, hands, feet, and mouth to You. Lord, I pray that I will be in perfect peace with You so my soul and spirit prosper in You. Father, I accept all Your instructions, help me to walk in obedience and lay up Your words in my heart. Lord, You are my God and I thank You for loving me in spite of me and my flaws. Teach me to do Your will to bring You glory in my actions and in the words I speak in Jesus' name, Amen.

Putting on the Whole Armor of God

(Ephesians 6:10-19 NIV)

God, I come to You asking You to forgive me for all of my sins. Lord everything I have said done or thought that was a sin please forgive me. God, I thank You for another day to be able to come before You and bless Your holy awesome name. Lord thank You for making me strong in You and in the power of Your might. I put on the whole armor of God that I will be able to stand against the schemes of the devil. I do not wrestle against flesh and blood but against the rulers, authorities, and powers of this world's darkness and against the spiritual powers of evil in the spiritual world. I put on the helmet of salvation, the breastplate of righteousness, I gird my loins with the belt of truth and shod my feet with the word of peace that will help me stand strong. I have in my hand the shield of faith to quench every fiery dart of the devil. I take up the sword of the Spirit which is Your word that I will be able to stand and having done all I will stand strong and when the fight is finished I will still be standing. God, I will pray in the Spirit at all times with all kinds of prayers asking You Lord for everything I need. I ask You to strengthen me so that I have easy victories knowing that if You be for me who can be against me in Jesus name. Help me to stay ready and never give up and to continually pray for Your people. Thank You Jehovah Nissi my Banner for raising up a standard over me. Thank You, Lord, for the Whole Armor of God and the skills to use it in Jesus' name, Amen.

A Prayer of Repentance

(Acts 3:19 NIV)

Father in the name of Jesus I come to You with a repented heart. I ask You, Lord, to forgive me for every one of my sins, anything I've said, done, thought, or didn't do that You commanded me to do Lord forgive me. I repent Lord for being disobedient in the things I say and do. I repent for not living my life according to Your Word. Father, You are such a gracious and kind Father, please give me another chance to get it right with You in Jesus name. Father, I am a mess and I need You to help me. God, I am turning to You for You to wipe out all of my sins that a time of refreshing may come from You Lord. Fill me with more of you God, show me Your glory! I love You Father and trust You. My faith lays only in You. You are the God of my salvation and I thank You in Jesus' name, Amen.

A Prayer of Forgiveness

(Matthew 6:14-15 NIV)

God, I come to You in the name of Jesus asking You Lord to forgive me. God, You said in Your word that if I forgive people when they sin against me that You my Heavenly Father will be faithful to forgive me. Father, I let go of every grudge, every hurt, and every lie that's been told to me or on me. Lord, I even forgive myself for hurting others and myself. Forgiving

my self is a hard thing to do because I
have to live with myself so Father,
help me to lay everything at Your feet
and release it all to You. I ask You,
God, to cover me with the blood of
Jesus and renew in me a clean heart
that I may be able to serve You in
excellence and let everything I do be
pleasing to You and glorify You in
Jesus' name, Amen.

Walking in Wisdom

(Ephesians 5:14-16 & James 1:5 NIV)

God, I come to You asking You to
forgive me for all of my sins. Lord
everything I have said done or thought
that was a sin please forgive me.
Father in the name of Jesus I come
before You asking You for wisdom.

You said in You word James 1:5 that if I lack wisdom to ask You and You will generously give me wisdom without fault. Lord, give me wisdom generously in Jesus' name. Father, You are my light and You make everything visible to me in Jesus' name. Take the scales off my eyes that I will see all that You are doing in my life. Awaken my spirit that I will not be spiritually dead but that Christ will be my light. Guide me God that I will live a holy life careful to follow You. Help me Lord not to live like a fool but to live wisely in the name of Jesus, Amen.

Make me wiser than my enemies

(Psalm 119:98 NIV)

Father, in the mighty and powerful name of Jesus I come to You asking You to forgive me for all of my sins Lord. Forgive me for everything I have said done and thought that wasn't pleasing to You Lord. I plead the blood of Jesus over myself and I put on the whole armor of God on today. Lord, I come asking You to make me wiser than my enemies that I will not be deceived or taken by surprise by their evil ways. Father, give me insight into their plans and give me an understanding of what to do and when to do it. Father, I bind up the works, the plans and the plots that my enemies are trying to do against me and my family. Lord, I thank You that it will not work. I ask You Lord to return to my enemies every lie, plot, plan, and trick they have set out against me or my family that my enemies will fall into their own traps and be found guilty in Jesus' name. Father, show me who to avoid show me who is for me and who is against me that I would not be made a fool out of by my enemies. In Jesus' name, I pray, Amen.

Pride & Humility

(Proverbs 11:2 NIV)

God, I come to You asking You to forgive me for all of my sins. Lord everything I have said done or thought that was a sin please forgive me. Father in the name of Jesus I come before You as humble as I know how asking You Lord to empty me of any pride that may cause me to be disgraced. I ask You, God, to empty me and search my heart of everything that is not like You. Lord, You said in Proverbs 11:2 that "Pride leads to disgrace but with humility comes wisdom". Father clothed me with humility and pour wisdom generously into me. Don't let my heart be hardened by pride but let my heart be in pursuit of You Lord. You, Father, are my guide help me to continue to follow the steps You have for me that I do not get ahead of You but that I stay right in Your will and in Your perfect timing in the name of Jesus, Amen.

Keep Me Close God

(Ecclesiastes 12:13 & Proverbs 9:10 NIV)

Father, I come to You asking You to forgive me for all of my sins. Lord everything I have said done or thought that was a sin please forgive me. Heavenly Father, in the name of Jesus I ask You to keep me in Your will that I continue to fear You because Proverbs 9:10 says that the fear of the Lord is the beginning of wisdom and knowledge of the Holy One is understanding. Help me keep Your commandments for this is the duty You gave every man. Lord, I draw nigh to You continue to draw nigh to me in Jesus' name. Don't allow me to drift away from You God. You are everything I need, my guide, my

deliverer, my daily source, and my all
in all. I need You, Father, continue to
make me whole in You. Thank You,
Father, that I am close to You and
know Your voice and a stranger's
voice I will not follow in Jesus' name,
Amen.

Giving it all to You Lord

(Romans 12:1-2 NIV)

Abba Father, I come to You thanking
You for the great mercies You have
shown me. I present to You my life,
my sleeping, my eating, my working,
my husband and marriage, the raising
of my children, and my relationships.
Lord, my life is Yours, let it be pleasing
to You and worship to You. Lord, I will
not be conformed to this world but I

will be transformed by the renewing of my mind by You. Father, give me a new way of thinking so I will know what You God want for me and I will know what is good, pleasing and perfect to You Father in the name of Jesus...Amen

A Prayer When You're Weak

(Isaiah 40:28-29 NIV)

El Olam, my Ever Lasting God I come to You thanking You for being my Everlasting God, the Creator of everything in heaven and earth. The God that doesn't faint or get weary, the God whose understanding is unsearchable, the God who gives power to the weak and increases the strength of them who have no might.

El Olam I need You. I need You because I am weak and weary. I don't understand what is going on in my life. I need You to give me power, understanding, and strength. I praise You and thank You in advance for Your will being done in my life. In Jesus' Mighty Powerful Strong name, Amen.

A Prayer for Success

(Jeremiah 29:11 & I Kings 2:3 NIV)

Father, in the name of Jesus I come to You thanking You for Godly success. Lord, You said in Your word in Jeremiah 29:11 You know the plans You have for me. You declared that they are plans to prosper me and not to harm me and You have plans to give me hope and a future. Lord, You also said in I Kings 2:3 that if I observe what You require by walking in obedience to You and keeping Your decrees, commands, laws, and regulations that You will prosper me in all that I do and wherever I go. I will continue to humble myself before You Lord because You said You would exalt me in James 4:10. God, I commit my work to You that my plans will be established (Prov.16:3) and I will continually delight myself in You. Lord, I pray that You will give me the desires of my heart (Psalm 37:4). I thank You, God, for Godly success, direction, wisdom, knowledge, and love to do everything You have planned for me to do in life. In Jesus' name, I pray, Amen.

Help me when I'm Tested & Tempted

(I Corinthians 10:13 NIV)

Father, in the mighty name of Jesus I come to You asking You to forgive me for all of my sins. Lord, You are awesome in all of Your ways and I need You! I need Your Holy Spirit to help me when I'm faced with tests and temptations. Whether it's a conversation I shouldn't partake in, that place I shouldn't go, the curse word I let slip out now and then, or even that piece of chocolate cake I know I don't need. God help me have self-control and say no in Jesus' name! God help me to walk away from temptation and help me to stand still during the test. I know there is nothing I face in life that somebody else hasn't faced but I need Your strength to help me to live a life that makes You smile, filled with purpose, joy, peace, laughter, and love; the abundant life that is promised through Christ Jesus. Thank You, Father, for my prayers being answered in Jesus' name, Amen!

Side Chick & Cheaters

(Acts 3:19 NIV)

Father, in the name of Jesus I ask You to forgive me for having an affair with someone else's husband. Help me to drop him and let him go immediately in Jesus' name. I repent wholeheartedly and ask You, Father, to wash my mind from thoughts of him and I. Cleanse my heart from any feelings of love or lust I have towards him. Cleanse my spirit of all spiritual transference between the two of us. Wash my emotions of all the longing to be with him. Purge my body of anything that contaminated me from the sin of adultery. Lord, please help me to know my self-worth and see myself the way You see me. Help me Lord to be strong in You and have self-control. Lord I need You to make me whole because I am broken. Father, I pray that when You bring me, my husband that all the hurt I caused someone else's marriage I won't feel in mine because I understand the principles of reaping what I sow. Please have mercy on me Lord and forgive me. I surrender my desires to

You and I will wait on the husband that You have for me, in Jesus' name, Amen.

Prayer for someone married cheating on their spouse

(1 John 1:9 NIV)

Lord, forgive me today for everything I have done against Your word. I need a Savior right now! My heart is heavy Lord because I have been cheating on my spouse. Help me God to stop! Give me the strength to turn from my wicked ways and to work things out with my husband. Help me Lord to have self-control. I want to be led by Your Spirit not by my flesh in Jesus' name. Help me to stand on the principles of Your word and not on the things of this world. Lord, touch my husband's heart and mind and give him a spirit of forgiveness so that he will forgive me for hurting him. Lord, we need You to help us to fall back in love with each other that we will be attracted to each other physically, mentally, and spiritually. Touch my husband that he will love me the way Christ loves the church and touch me, Father, that I will adore and respect him all the days of our lives in Jesus' name, Amen.

A Prayer to Trust Again

(Psalm 9:10 NIV)

Lord, in the name of Jesus I ask You to forgive me for all of my sins and ask You to help me trust You with my life, husband, children, marriage, and finances. Help my unbelief in Your power for my life, my joy, and my peace. Help me to forgive my dad and my husband because they have hurt me deeply to my heart and I'm angry! I feel like I have been hurt by every man I was supposed to trust and I let my guard down to let into my life. Help me, Jesus! I feel like I can't trust anyone including You. El Olam my Everlasting Father I am wholeheartedly putting my trust in You right now in Jesus' name. Mend my broken heart, restore my joy, increase my peace and faith and help me to rest in You Lord. Father, You, are the only one that can put me back together again because I am broken and at times I feel shattered to the point I can't catch my breath. Help me I'm desperate for Your touch and restoration. Lord, Your word says that those who know Your name trust in You because You have never forsaken those who seek You in Jesus' powerful mighty name, Amen. Thank You, Lord I praise and glorify You!

A Prayer of Repentance

(2 Peter 3:9 NIV)

Father, in the name of Jesus I come to You asking for forgiveness of all of my sins. I accept Jesus as my Savior. I repent for not living my life in obedience to Your word. I repent for not trusting You with my life, family, finances, marriage, and career. I repent for not giving You my whole heart. I repent for thinking negative thoughts and cursing. I repent for not praying and reading the Bible daily. I repent for not going to church to hear Your word. I repent for looking and listening to things I shouldn't. Help me Lord to be strong enough to not gossip and be wise enough to know when to be quiet and still. Help me to not sin when I'm angry and to forgive quickly. Father be patient with me and continue to work on cleaning me up because I am a mess. In Jesus' powerful name I pray, Amen.

Send Me to Preach Your Word

(Mark 16:15-18 NIV)

Father, in the name of Jesus I come
before You asking You, Lord, to forgive
me for all my sins. Anything I have
said, done or even thought that was
not pleasing to You forgive me in the
name of Jesus. Lord, You say in Your
word Mark 16:15-18 "Go into all the
world and preach the gospel to every
creature he who believes." Lord, I
believe in Your word and in the power
of Your Holy Spirit. I ask You to use me
Lord, to minister to those who are lost
and need a Savior. Father, this world is
dying and confused not knowing the
truth from a lie. I give myself to You
Lord as a willing vessel to take Your
word to those in darkness whether
that is in the church building or on the

street send me to preach the Good News. Help me to preach with power and authority that Your word would penetrate the hearts and change the minds of the lost and hurting people. Lord, direct my path and my actions that I bring honor to Jesus Christ in all that I do. Lord, make me talk and walk in fearless courage that I will not be ashamed of the gospel of Jesus Christ no matter who rises up against me. I know that to die is gain but help me Father, to remain in the land of the living to share my faith in Jesus with all that will listen. Lord, take me to place no one else will go to talk to people no one else will talk to so I can share Your word with them in Jesus' name, Amen.

A Prayer of Adoption

(Romans 8:15 NIV)

Father, in the name of Jesus I come to You and ask You Lord to forgive me for all of my sins. Everything I've said, done or thought that wasn't pleasing to You forgive me, Lord. Lord, I need You to help me know who I am. Father, I don't know who my biological father is and I have felt like I have lost my identity at times. Lord, I know Your word says in Romans 8:15 that I did not receive a spirit of slavery that leads to fear but that I have received a spirit of adoption through Jesus Christ because it is Your pleasure and will. Lord, help me to keep my identity in You knowing that I am the daughter of the King of kings and Lord of lords. Father, help me to always remember that I am royalty a Powerful Praying Princess and that I have designer DNA and genes because of the Blood of Jesus. Take away the hurt from being abandoned and dropped by my birth parents and those who raised me and give me peace and perseverance to press forward knowing You, God, are my Abba Father, my good, good Father who loves me and whose royal DNA runs through my body and spirit in Jesus precious name I pray, Amen!

Prayer of Joy

(Psalm 119 NIV)

Lord, in the name of Jesus I come to You giving You praise and honor for joy. Lord, You, said in Psalm 119:1-2

that people are joyful that have
integrity and follow Your instructions.
Help me, Father, to continue to have
Godly integrity that my joy may be
seen by all I encounter everywhere I
go. Help me Lord to keep and follow
Your commandments day and night.
Father, I need You to keep me that I
obey Your laws and guard my heart
that I search for You wholeheartedly.
You, God, are my joy and strength and
I thank You. Your word is hidden in my
heart and I meditate on it day and
night. Lord, help me to be consistent
in my search of You through prayer,
fasting and reading Your word in
Jesus' name, Amen.

A Wife's Prayer for Her Husband and Family

(Ephesians 5:22-29 NIV)

God, I come to You in faith knowing that You are a God of order and excellence. I lift my marriage up to You and dedicate it back to You, oh God asking that Your will be done in it. Your word says that You have placed my husband as the head of our household the way Christ is the head of the church. I pray that my husband will love me the way Christ loves the church. Help us, God, not to rebel or have any misunderstood attitude toward the word or action of submitting but give both of us a good understanding of the word. God, touch my husband's heart that he submits to Your will and Your way for his life and family. God touch my husband that he will lead our household wisely. Help him to love me sacrificially because Your word says that he who loves his wife loves, nourishes, and cherishes himself just as Christ does the church because we are members of His body and my husband and I are one. Help me, God, to cover him in prayer, fast for him and respect him. Open up the lines of communication that we will pray together, seeking Your direction for our family. God, touch him to take charge of our worship time as a family giving honor to You for being El Shaddai the Almighty God. I thank You, Lord, God for Your will being done in Jesus mighty strong name, Amen.

A Prayer to be kept when in a drought

(Isaiah 58:11 NIV)

Father, in the mighty name of Jesus; forgive me Lord for all of my sins. I come to You God in the name above all names Jesus Christ asking You to guide me continually and to satisfy my soul during seasons of drought. Lord that neither I nor my household lack anything we need or desire. Lord, strengthen my bones that I am not weak physically, emotionally, or spiritually in the name of Jesus. Lord, make me to be like a watered garden whose fruits flourish even in drought and that's well-tended to and kept, whose weeds are plucked so they can't overtake the fruit. Lord keep me continually satisfied like a spring of water whose waters do not fall in Jesus' name, Amen.

Give Me the Gift of Tongues

(I Corinthians 14:4 NIV)

God, You also say in Mark 16:17 that the signs will follow those who believe in my name they will cast out demons. God, I ask You give me the strength, the knowledge, power, and authority to cast out demons. You also say in Mark 16:17 that they will speak with new tongues. Lord, I ask that You to give me the gifts of speaking and interpreting tongues. Lord Mark 16:18 says they will lay hands on the sick and they will recover. God, send a fresh anointing to my holy hands to do Your will for Your glory and Your namesake in Jesus' name. Father Your word also says in I Corinthians 14:4 "He who speaks in a tongue edifies himself." Lord, I want to edify myself by speaking in tongues so Father in the name of Jesus I claim and receive all of these things in Jesus' name, Amen.

A prayer for my words to please God

(Psalm 19:14 NIV)

Father, in the name of Jesus I come to You asking You to forgive me. Lord, forgive me for every sarcastic, judgmental, complaining, negative, gossiping, hurtful word I have said and thought about myself or someone else in Jesus' name. Lord, I am asking You to bridle my tongue on today that I do not speak words that are harmful to me or others. Help me to avoid conversations that are gossiping and useless in Jesus' name. Help me God to close my mouth so I don't sin with my words. Help me to listen to You and to get guidance in my conversations with each person I come in contact with today. Help me to hear what I need to hear even if they are complaining or negative give me the insight to see the hurt and address the hurt behind their words. Lord, help me not to be sarcastic or judgmental but to give me wisdom and insight to speak edifying words of peace and love. Lord, You, know I can be sarcastic and it comes out so quickly and easy please help me to shut my mouth. I thank You Lord in Jesus' name, Amen.

A prayer for God to abide in me

(John 15:1-16 NIV)

Father, I come to You knowing that You are the true giver of life. I ask You Lord to cut off everyone and everything that distracts me from producing the fruits You want me to produce. Purify my heart, mind, thoughts, motives, and intentions and help me to remain in Your will for my life. Lord, please remain in me and continue to draw me closer to You. Father, direct me in how to bring You great glory. Lord, I know I need discipline and help to be obedient to Your commandments and to walk in love. Fill me with Your joy and love until it is overflowing. Teach me, Lord, how to love those people who are unlovable the same way You love them, God You know the people that have no love or knowledge of You. I thank You, Lord for choosing me and appointing me to produce lasting fruit. Thank You, Father, for answering my prayers and letting Your will be done in my life. In Jesus' name, I pray, Amen.

Let the angel of the Lord persecute my enemies

(Ephesians 6:12 NIV)

Father, I come to You asking You to let Your angels fight for me and my family in the heavens against principalities,

powers, rulers of the darkness and
spiritual wickedness in high places.
Have Your angels to go before my
children and make the crooked places
straight (Zechariah 12:8). Send Your
angels to smite the demons that come
to destroy me and my family in Jesus'
name. Lord, I bind and rebuke all
people and enemies that have plotted
against me and my family. I bind up
and rebuke spirits of hatred, murder,
premature death and suicidal
thoughts that try to manifest in my
family through witchcraft and
manipulation I return them to the
sender in Jesus' name, Amen.

Lord contend with my enemies

(Psalm 35 NIV)

Lord, You said in Your word that You would contend with those who contend with me and that You will fight those who fight against me. I need You, Lord, to contend and fight with those that are against me. Come to my aid Lord and disgrace and put to shame people who try to harm me and my family. Father, confuse everyone that has plots and plans to ruin me and my family. Lord, I pray that my enemies will be like chaff in the wind and Your angels force them away. Father, darken and make slippery the paths of my enemies as Your angels chase them. I thank You that the blood of Jesus covers me and

my family and is against my enemies
in Jesus' mighty name, Amen.

Save my Children

(Acts 16:31, NIV)

Father, in the awesome name of Jesus
I come to You lifting up my children.
Lord Your word says that if I believe in
the Lord Jesus I will be saved and my
household will be saved. God save my
children's souls in Jesus name. I give
them to You God Your will is for them
to prosper and be in good health as
their souls prosper. Their souls can't
prosper unless they are in You, so
deliver them and save them out of the
hand of the enemy who is trying to sift
them as wheat. Show my children
their purpose so that they can live

their lives doing Your will and walking in obedience to You. Thank You, Father, for Your grace and mercy in their lives and please continue to cover them with the Blood of Jesus and encamp Your heavenly angels around them keeping them safe from dangers seen and unseen and even from themselves in Jesus' name, Amen.

Lord fight for me

(Exodus 14:13-14, NIV)

Lord, I stand here knowing that Your word says I am not to be afraid but to stand firm and I will see You deliver me today. Father, it is hard to be still right now and wait on You. Help me to not try to fix this situation myself but give me the strength to stand and continue to wait on You Lord. I am weak Lord but I know You're my strength. I bind up the lies of the enemy that would have me think that You have forgotten me and I praise You in advance for my victory! As I continue to be still Lord while You fight for me in Jesus' name, Amen.

Dedicated to Pastor Spence & my GICM family

Promotion of the Gospel of Jesus Christ

(Romans 1:16, NIV)

God, I come to You asking You to forgive me for all of my sins. Lord, everything I have said done or thought that was a sin please forgive me.

Father, in the name of Jesus I ask You to equip me for the Promotion of the Gospel of Jesus Christ. I am not ashamed of the Gospel because it is Your power God that brings salvation to everyone who believes. Give me the understanding of Your word to be able to correctly explain the word of truth. I am not ashamed to minister Your word to those who are lost and hungry for Your truth. God, I present myself to You as Your vessel to use me at Your will. In Jesus' name, Amen.

A Passion for the Power & Presence of God

(Acts 1:8 NKJV)

God, I come to You asking You to forgive me for all of my sins. Lord, everything I have said done or thought that was a sin please forgive me. Lord I come to You asking You Father to empty me out so You can fill me with Your Holy Spirit. I need more of YOU LORD. God, decrease me so that You can increase in me. I surrender to You God that the Holy Spirit may come dwell in me that I can receive the power that You promise in Acts 1:8 so that I may be a witness for Jesus Christ to all You direct me to. God, I need Your power and anointing to go forth in You! God, give me a passion for the power and presence of God like no other. Show me Your glory God in Jesus' name, Amen.

A Preoccupation with Prayer

(I Thessalonians 5:17 NKJV)

Father in the mighty name of Jesus I come before You humbly asking You to forgive me, Lord. I need You to guide my prayers, Lord. Teach me how to pray. Show me what to pray and who to pray for. Lord, I desire to pray without ceasing being preoccupied with prayer day and night no matter where I am and what I'm doing. God, quicken in me a deeper stronger prayer life that I make time to commune with You in the name of Jesus. Father, touch my church family that Global Impact Christian Ministries be taken to another level in prayer that we as a whole be preoccupied with prayer and never cease communing with You in Jesus' name, Amen.

Dedicated to Pastor Spence & my GICM family

A Proliferation of Praise

(Psalm 100, NKJV)

God, I come to You asking You to forgive me for all of my sins. Lord everything I have said done or thought that was a sin please forgive me. Lord, I shout with joy to You because You are the Lord of all the earth! I worship You Lord with gladness and come before You singing with joy. I know that You Lord are my God! You have made me and I am Yours. I enter into Your gates with thanksgiving and enter Your courts with praise. I thank You and praise Your Holy name because You Lord are good and your unfailing love continues forever and Your faithfulness continues to each generation. Thank You, God, for being God and touching us at Global Impact Christian Ministries teaching us how to have a proliferation of praise for You in the name of Jesus......Amen.

A Practice of Living What You Preached

(James 1:22, NKJV)

Lord, please forgive me for my sins, the things I have said done and didn't do that You told me to do please forgive me. Father in the mighty name of Jesus I come to You asking You to help me not just be a listener of Your word but to also do what Your word says to do. Help me God to follow the instructions that You have given me and to keep each commandment in Your word. Lord, I thank You that if and when I fall short You are merciful to forgive and give me another chance to get it right with You. I don't want to be a fool but I want to be intelligent in

You and Your word. Father, give my pastor, Pastor Spence the strength and words to teach my GICM family each week. Bless him and his family to do Your will and to live according to Your word, free from scandal, chaos, and foolishness. Thank You, Lord, that we practice what we preach in Jesus' name.... Amen.

Dedicated to Pastor Spence & my GICM family

A Partnership with the Local Community

(Acts 4:32-35 NKJV)

Lord, forgive me for all of my sins. I praise and glorify You on today because You are a faithful, loving, giving God. Heavenly Father I come before You asking You Lord to unite the Body of Christ here in Stockbridge, McDonough, and all of Henry County and Metro Atlanta that we will be united in heart and mind. Help us to all work toward the goal of helping the communities, that there would be no household in need of anything because You supply all needs according to Your riches in glory through Christ Jesus. Lord, I thank You that GICM partners with our local communities and make a godly impact through blessing all You put in our path. I thank You, Lord, that You are making the government aware of the impact GICM is making and I thank You that senators, commissioners, mayors, and governors will know our name and integrity, ethics, blessings, excellence, and favor will be attached to GICM! God, I thank You that they will bless us to be a blessing and cause them to give to GICM in the name of Jesus.....Amen.

Dedicated to Pastor Spence & my GICM family

A Priority of Global Outreach

(Matthew 28:19 NKJV)

Father, in the name of Jesus, prepare GICM to go out into the neighborhoods, towns, cities, states, and nations to teach and preach Your word to every person we meet. Lord that people will be saved and baptized in the name of the Father, Son, and Holy Spirit. Help us to teach others how to live by Your word in Jesus' name. Father, equip us to be overcomers by the blood of the Lamb and the word of our testimonies not having fear to share our testimonies because we are overcomers through Christ Jesus the ultimate overcomer. Thank You, Lord, in Jesus' name, Amen!

The Powerful Praying Princesses LLC

Our Mission is to intercede for our nation, leaders, pastors, the Body of Christ, friends, family, enemies, & anyone that asks us to pray for them.

Please join us for prayer

M-F 5:30am-5:45am & 7days a week 9:30pm-10pm

515-603-4924 access code 257640#

References

Hagin, Kenneth <u>Foundations of Faith,</u> USA: Faith Library
  Publications, 1998 page 5

Munroe, Myles <u>Understanding the Purpose and Power of
  Prayer Earthly License for Heavenly Interference.</u>
  USA: Whitaker House, 2002 page 65

<u>The King James Study Bible.</u> USA: Thomas Nelson, Inc. 1988

<u>The Holy Bible New International Version,</u> USA: Zondervan,
  2011

Made in the USA
Coppell, TX
02 May 2022

77337342R00215